Schools
– of –
Old Poole

by

Doreen E W Young

South Road and Others

1628 – 1995

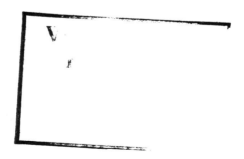

POOLE HISTORICAL TRUST
1996

Previous Publications
The Pride of Poole, 1688-1851
An Album of Old Poole
Mansions and Merchants of Poole and Dorset
Brownsea Islander
Poole and World War II
Portfolio of Old Poole
Ebb-Tide at Poole
History of the Town of Poole, 1839 (reprint)
The Sydenhams of Poole (booklet)
Art in Poole and Dorset
Victorian Poole
Poole after World War II 1945-1953
D-Day Poole (booklet)
The Spirit of Poole 1953-1963
Lifeboatmen Never Turn Back

Copyright © Doreen E W Young 1996
First published 1996
ISBN 1 873535 25 2

Revised and enlarged version of
Schools of Old Poole - South Road and Before - 1628-1980
published 1980 by Polus Press (ISBN 0 907 296 00 9)

Edited and prepared for publication by Ian Andrews.
Designed by Graham M Smith and Andrew S Arnold.
Production and film by Graphic Editions, Poole.
Printed and bound in Great Britain by Biddles Limited, Guildford and King's Lynn.

Dedicated to the Schoolchildren of Poole

Past, Present and Future.

Especially

NIGEL and GILLIAN, JAMIE, NICHOLAS,

THOMAS and JOANNE

Acknowledgements

The author would like to thank:

Mr A.N. Kellaway B.Ed.(Hons), Headmaster of South Road School for loan of School Records - and his Staff.

The Staff, Librarians and ex-Staff of the schools involved, especially Nick Latcham, Anne Batley, Marion Watson, Ken Corio, Terry Gillingham, Joy Randall, Mrs Greaves, Mrs Jordan and Mrs Criscuolo.

Poole Museum Service.

All the many Poole folk who so willingly offered photos, school magazines and documents. My great regret is that all could not be used.

Contents

Preface

The actual second of decision to attempt the story of South Road School came as I examined for the umpteenth time the seven garments made by my Mother - Vera Elaine Whittaker - at South Road School in 1912 under the supervision of Miss Buckmaster. The details, for example Girl's Chemise half size or Girl's Drawers half size, were written in that unmistakeable handwriting of the time by my Mother on each garment - for they are made of sepia coloured tissue paper! Every detail is perfect, the gathers (so evenly stroked), the tucks, the hems, the buttonholes, the buttons even, the turnings, the lace edgings - all and everything made of paper.

Surely, I thought to myself, the School responsible for such a production must be unique, the story worth telling. And so it came to pass that I picked up the telephone and spoke to Mr Kellaway, the Headmaster of the day, of my intentions. His enthusiasm then, in 1979, encouraged me to produce the first "Schools of Old Poole".

And now in 1995 we learn that the Old School in its present form is to go. Those paper garments which inspired me to start on the history have long been in the safe keeping of Poole Museum as was my Mother's wish before she died early in 1982.

The children of the Old Town will have a brand new modern school to attend at Tatnam in 1997. I can only hope future generations will hold that establishment in such loving esteem as did past pupils of South Road.

DOREEN E W YOUNG

Introduction

To look at South Road School from either South Road (the Boys' side) or from Green Road (the Girls' side) one sees a stolid two-storey building of sandy beige bricks topped by a dark red roof, still in excellent condition and much as it was when built in 1911 on the site of the old Poole Iron Foundry.

A small playground either side has since been enlarged by the inclusion of ground which was previously the site of Butler's Brush Factory. The walls which used to separate the Boys from the Girls are now gone. And there it is, an ordinary rather uninteresting-looking school building by any standards.

The emotive reaction to the words South Road School by anyone connected in any way to the school of whatever age is quite extraordinary.

My quest to trace the beginnings of this pillar of Education led me back through very unexpected and interesting ways and it is no wonder that a building with such a motley ancestry should have turned out the way it has.

When I started out on this journey towards the end of 1978 I never envisaged having to retrace steps as far back as 1628 to the first Free School built by the then Mayor, Thomas Robarts in Thames Street opposite St James Church. Ironically (and that's not meant to be a pun) Poole Iron Foundry then stood on that site.

Kindness, compassion, generosity, greed, dissension and power all took their turn and it would be quite impossible if not unkind to jump from Thames Street in 1628 to South Road in 1912 without a mention of the events between and without tracing the growth of Education by means of the Schools provided by the Churches and Chapels in Old Poole.

The education provided by these Church Sunday Schools was meagre but it was something for the many underprivileged children who lived in the Old Town. And these establishments provided the foundations for the Schools which were to follow.

The mother church of St James played its part but due to the very strong Nonconformist attitude of the majority of the Townspeople, the Established Church Schools for a time were outnumbered.

Even at the turn of the century many of the wealthy Nonconformist Poole gentlemen opposed the Government legislation to the extent that they refused to pay rates which may have been used to support Church of England Schools. This led to a strong line of action in that the Town Bailiffs were sent to procure their silver or other valuables in custody until such time as the said rates were paid.

By the time South Road was built in 1911, the elementary schools of Poole seemed to be working on a basis of cooperation and friendly rivalry.

In this revised edition of my earlier book I have extended the text to cover the Secondary Schools which most impinge on the Old Town and this story is also not without its controversies.

Opposite: map of Poole showing the sites of the 'Schools of Old Poole'

Free School	–	1
St James	–	2
Boys' National School	–	3
Girls' National School	–	4
Chapel Lane Infants' (1st Rattrays)	–	5
St Pauls Infants' School	–	6
British School	–	7
Lagland Street Infants' School (Rattrays)	–	8
St Mary's Roman Catholic School	–	9
South Road School	–	10
Poole Secondary School	–	11
Poole Grammar/Seldown School	–	12
Henry Harbin School	–	13

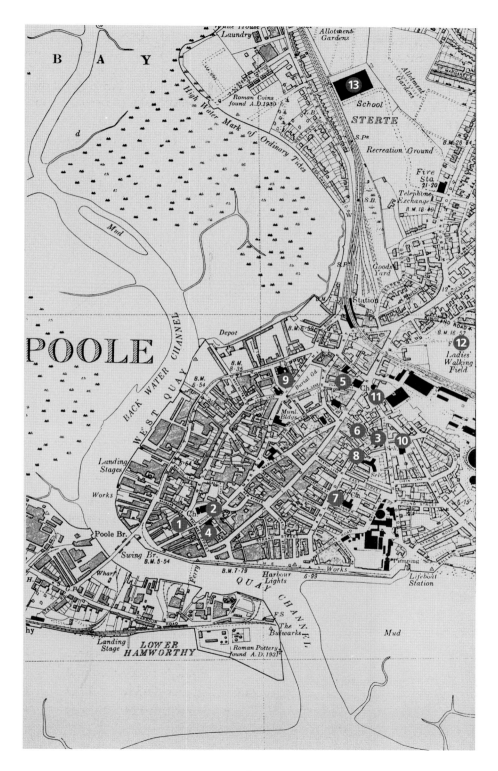

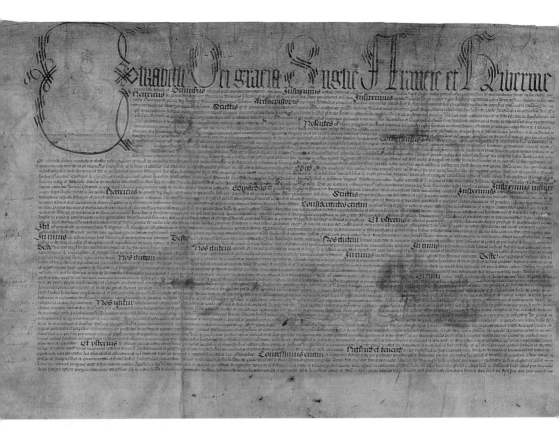

The Great Charter of Queen Elizabeth I granting to Poole the status of a County Corporate.
This valuable document is deposited in the Poole Borough Archive.

Beginnings

I n the year 1568 Queen Elizabeth I granted a Charter to Poole raising its status to that of a County Corporate. No doubt enthused by this significant event, the Burgesses of the day were not lacking in ideas to improve the services of the town.

A request made when seeking the Charter was that an annuity, previously paid to Cardinal Pole, should henceforth be reallocated for the maintenance of a Free School in Poole. At the earliest opportunity education was being given serious thought at what would now be described as "Town Hall level", even if it was only to ensure that the wealthy merchants who ran the town could give their sons and heirs a better chance in life than they had enjoyed. Learning to read and speak Latin was in those days essential to any sort of social standing.

The idea was obviously unacceptable for the Charter was silent on the matter. Perhaps the endowment was considered insufficient or unacceptable. For one thing, Poole lacked a cathedral or monastery to which a school was traditionally attached.

The town eventually acted on its own, for in 1628 Thomas Robarts, Mayor of the day, built a Free School opposite St. James' Church in Thames Street on a site later occupied by Poole Iron Foundry (since demolished and now covered by a housing development, Barbers Wharf). It was not unreasonable that the foundation stone of the school should be inscribed with the initials of the Robarts family with the date, June 1628. This foundation stone survived more than two hundred years to be given a memorial position within the National School at Perry Gardens. Early in the 17th century George Trenchard had bequeathed £6 a year towards maintaining a Grammar School. Isaac Turner was the first Master.

Attendance at the Free or Grammar School attracted a great deal of prestige as, from all accounts, it was a very good school. It included the teaching of writing (by no means usual at this date), and navigation also formed part of the regular syllabus. The twenty two pupils were mainly the sons of shipowners and leading tradesmen and they acquired a free place by selection. This was in the hands of the Mayor, who received recommendations from people of good standing in the town. Thus the diary of Benjamin Lester (then Mayor) records on 14th December 1779: *"Gave Mr Colbourne an order to take in Joseph Dean's son into the Free School by recommendation of Mr John Bird, Junior."* Mr Colbourne, a freemason, was the Schoolmaster from 1768 to 1786 and the town's two MP's met his salary. John Bird had been Mayor three years earlier.

The Free School lacked a formal foundation document and the arrangements are therefore vague.The Borough appears to have met the expenses, at least partly, from rents received from charities set up under the wills of Henry Harbin and John Bennett. The Schoolmaster often held the post in a dual appointment, being also the vestry clerk, Rector or attorney. The school survived (with a fire occurring in 1763) until 1835, when the National School in Perry Gardens succeeded it.

For those not among the select and privileged few, the only hint of education was gleaned by attending catechism at church. This was also restrictive because the only place of religion in Poole until the 17th century was St. James. Nevertheless, whilst it may have formed part of the community ritual, attendance at church was then of greater consequence than it is today. In view of the influence of the church, the development of the schooling system cannot be revealed in isolation from the activities of the churches. From the 1780's the work of Robert Raikes at Gloucester had led to a rapid spread of Sunday Schools teaching religion, but also reading, to all children. None were to be regarded as too poor, neglected, dirty or ragged to be admitted.

In the early days, the parish of St. James was also the town boundary and St. James, although the Established Church and the only place of religion, tended to adopt a Nonconformist policy. During the middle part of the 17th century, the first signs of a Dissenting congregation are noticed. This situation appears to have arisen from the pastoral activities of a Reverend John Wesley, son of a Mr Bartholomew Wesley of Charmouth, grandfather of the celebrated founder of Wesleyan Methodism. Revd John Wesley although said to be residing in Preston, near Weymouth, was called upon by a group of serious Poole Christians to act as their Pastor. This he did until his death, but not unhindered. Several times John Wesley was apprehended and four times imprisoned.

Poole's majority Nonconformist element was able to exercise influence even in the Established Church of St. James. Aldermen and members of the Town Council were obliged to take communion at the Established Church at least once a month, and as these men were ratepayers and more wealthy members of the town, they held a great deal of power. The Borough Council elected both the Rector of St. James and the Schoolmaster of the Free School to their positions. The Toleration Act of 1689 made it easier for Nonconformists to develop dissenting worship and for the royal peculiar of St James, from which Charles II had ousted Reverend Samuel Hardy, (a "hired nonconformist preacher"), from office in 1682, to become the stronghold of the Established Church. It established its Sunday School in rooms in the church tower in 1789.

The Nonconformists chose to move elsewhere and found churches of their own. Their first Sunday School predated St. James by at least two years. Wherever there was a church or a chapel, so the elders were keen to educate

St. James Church (demolished 1819)

the children of their own congregations.

The Dissenting congregation of St. James appeared to have been attracted first to Hill Street. It is here that the Presbyterian Meeting House was founded, and in 1655 was presided over by William Bayly (of Baptist inclination) who a year later joined the Quakers. In 1656 under Mr George Fox the Quakers established the Society of Friends' Meeting House in Lagland Street. The Baptist followers of William Bayly continued to worship in Hill Street until the opening of the new Baptist Chapel off West Butts Street. This building was donated to the Baptist element in 1735 by John Bird, who was later to become Mayor of Poole. Because of differences of opinion, this place of worship languished, and around 1790 was pulled down and the site used some years later as a Baptist burying ground. Some of the congregation worshipped in a little Meeting House off Carter's Lane, others joined the Congregationalists in Skinner Street until 1804 when Mr Joseph Saunders called the Baptist element together in order to start afresh with new covenants. For some time meetings were held at private houses in Dear Hay Lane and in Market Street (now Burt & Vick's). However, on Christmas Day 1806, a small chapel was opened in Bowling Green Alley. From that date the congregation thrived to the extent that a larger Baptist Chapel was built in Hill Street and opened in 1815. Whilst this was taking place, a Baptist Sunday School commenced in 1810.

The Great Presbyterian Meeting House, also in Hill Street, was built in the garden of Richard Burkman in 1705. This was later to become the

Wesleylan Chapel, High Street.

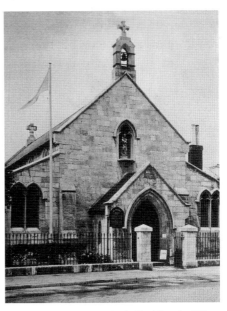

St. Mary's Roman Catholic Church, West Quay Road.

Unitarian Chapel. Yet more differences of opinion arose, and the seceding portion of the congregation of the Great Presbyterian Meeting House in 1760 under Reverend Samuel Phillips built a small Congregational Chapel in Lagland Street at the corner of Skinner Street. It is interesting that among the individuals who seceded to Lagland Street Congregational Chapel in 1760, was Martin Kemp, grandfather of Mr Martin Kemp-Welch whose name is now perpetuated in one of our schools. Under Revd S. Phillips, and especially his successor, Reverend Edward Ashburner, M.A., the Chapel flourished to the extent that when the new Congregational Chapel was built in Skinner Street in 1777, the old chapel was used for teaching and a formal Sunday School was in existence in 1787, later becoming the British School.

In 1793 the Wesleyan Methodist Chapel in Chapel Lane was built by J. H. Knight. The Sunday School superintendent in 1841 was Mr J. Hill (a shoemaker who owned a shop in Poole High Street). A day school was started there in 1884 by Isabel Rattray, and later transferred to Lagland Street Infants' School.

In 1839 the Roman Catholic Church of St. Mary's, West Quay Road, was erected and supported its own school on the premises. The new Catholic School was built to accommodate 120 children in 1850, but Miss Elizabeth Courtney, Mistress, reported an average attendance of only 86 in later years.

Old Poole was expanding rapidly. There had been a 25% increase in population between 1821 and 1831 and a new Anglican Church - St. Paul's - was erected in High Street in 1833. The Municipal Corporations' Act of

1835 resulted in the Borough extending to embrace Hamworthy, Parkstone and Longfleet, each with their respective schools following in due course.

Attendance at the Old Town Schools in 1835 was reported as:

St James'	192	Skinner Street	413
Baptists	74	Unitarian	19

Longfleet Workhouse (to replace the small one in West Street), built in 1835 for 170 inmates, also provided its own school with a Miss Annie M. Taylor as School Mistress. The Primitive Methodists, who originally met in a house in Cinnamon Lane, erected their new church in North Street in 1842 (this was re-built in 1896, the original foundation stones now being incorporated in the Wesleyan Methodist Chapel in Chapel Lane). In 1878 the new Wesleyan Chapel in High Street was built.

For most of the 19th century the schools of Poole struggled to cope with increasing demand. In the era of Reform and a widened franchise, after 1833 there were modest grants for school building, but the idea that the state should help provide education was only gradually accepted. Its attempts to intervene also caused much inter-denominational jealousy and strife. Fees charged to parents did not cover costs and as Poole's economy was going through hard times (the Borough Council went bankrupt), it was natural that any fit child was under pressure to earn a living at an early age. For most girls the only secular education they received was at home in preparation for domestic service and marriage. Full time free elementary education was not to be achieved until the present century, but increasing interest was being shown by the State in regulating standards, inspecting schools and training teachers. The 1870 Education Act finally set up a dual framework of School Boards and Church Schools, which brought some elementary education within the reach of all children. This was further refined in the 1902 Education Act, which gave county councils responsibility for secondary, and borough councils for

Old Wesleyan School Room in Chapel Lane, used for many years as Young Citizen's House.

elementary, education. The voluntary church schools became eligible for rate aid for the first time, but had to finance structural alterations and extensions themselves. With ageing buildings their Managers faced an increasingly difficult task.

The schools emanating from the Established Church were termed **National**, and those from the Nonconformist section **British**. In theory, at least, the two types of schools had differing methods of instruction and the classrooms were differently set out.

The **National** Schools were conducted upon the principles of the Church of England by the National Society for the Education of the Poor (established in 1811) throughout England and Wales. In National Schools there were normally two sets of desks capable of accommodating up to half the school in attendance. One set was placed three deep against the wall, and the other set formed a gallery for all instructions. Desks occupied only half the floor space and the rest was left clear for the children to stand in open squares and receive instruction.

The children at **British** Schools were taught in semi-circles. Apart from the teacher's desk and the gallery at one end of the schoolroom, all desks were placed in the centre, freeing surrounding spaces for group instruction. Some British Schools qualified for an annual grant, a small one, if they satisfied the Government Inspectors. Funds also came from the wealthier members of the congregation, from the British and Foreign Bible Society (established 1814), the Wesleyan Education Committee, and the children themselves were obliged to subscribe a penny, or maybe two pennies, a week towards their education.

For specialist subjects and for those able to afford them there were private schools and academies. Pigot's *Directory of Dorset* and Hunt and Co.'s *Dorsetshire Directory* listed some eight to ten private schools in the early 1800's. James Stephen, the great-great-grandfather of Virginia Woolf, wrote a telling insight into one of these. For a short while he and his brother attended a Boarding School run by Revd Howell at what was then the top of Lagland Street at Perry Gardens. *"Mr Howell's qualifications and habits as a teacher were probably not above par. Discipline was very lax. I remember being punished once only for neglect of school studies. I was improved a great deal in reading, to which a laudable attention was paid. As to Latin, any progress was very small. A subject far more interesting than school studies was my Master's eldest daughter, with whom, tho' I was scarcely more than ten years old, I fell desperately in love."*

Another Poole pupil, destined for fame as a naturalist, was Philip Henry Gosse. Philip first attended two small Dame schools at the lower end of the town before joining, in 1818, the educational establishment run by Mr Charles Henry Sells, a tall, agreeable man and a most efficient schoolmaster. Philip recalled wearing corduroy trousers and a moleskin jacket to school and enjoyed joining in the various games which the children were able to play in the near traffic-free streets of the time. Particular favourites were scourge-tops, peg-tops and humming-tops and marbles, played with marble-alleys, soap-alleys, "stoners" and the inferior "clayers".

The small private schools catered for the middle class and were set up separately for boys and girls. Some were day schools and some of them took boarders. A John Hosier, of Cinnamon Lane, had a grand sounding "Gentlemen's Commercial Boarding School". This elderly gentleman who had "knocked about the world a great deal in a rough way" offered teaching of writing, ciphering and navigation. One might assume he had spent his younger days at sea and had come to Poole to impart his nautical skills. However, his grammar was found lacking in the flourished penmanship specimen he displayed in a local shop window:

"These are sweet little cherubs what sits up aloft

To keep watch for the life of poor Jack."

Robert Baker taught music in Old Orchard, William Waller miniature paintings in Hill Street, and Thomas Wadham drawing at Baiter. Apart from these numerous small private schools or academies, as they were listed in Pigot's Directory, Poole also boasted a School of Art. This was first situated at the lower end of High Street, and later in the Public Free Library Building in Mount Street. Edwin Roland Gill was master at the time of the move, and R. Belben the secretary.

By 1899, St. James' No. 2 Infants' School opened in Perry Gardens at the corner of Globe Lane in the St Paul's School Sunday School premises (briefly Barbarella's Night Club prior to demolition). The old British School held for so many years in the Wesleyan Chapel, Chapel Lane, had occupied new premises in Lagland Street since 1894. This school seemed always to take the name of the first Headmistress, for many knew it only as "Rattray's".

From the original St. James' Sunday School in Old Poole there were now four main schools in operation in addition to St Mary's Roman Catholic School; St. James' Girls' National School (plus its No. 2 Infants' Section at Globe Lane), the Boys' National at Perry Gardens, the British School in Skinner Street, and Lagland Street Infants' (originally Chapel Lane Infants'). Each had its own little story to tell, before we reach the other schools of the Old Town, and so we return to St. James.

Poole National Schools.

ESTABLISHED 1835.

Under Annual Inspection by the Inspectors of the Privy Council, and the Salisbury Diocesan Board of Education.

PRESIDENT—The REV. A. WILKINSON.

TREASURER—Mr. G. BELBEN, Jun. | SECRETARY—Mr. G. H. GUTCH.

COMMITTEE.

The Rev. G. MORGAN | Mr. H. W. DICKINSON
Mr. E. LACY | Mr. W. L. C. ADEY
Mr. G. LEDGARD | Mr. R. HOSKINS
Mr. J. GOSSE |

MASTER—MR. W. P. STICKLAND.

PUPIL TEACHERS—F. STICKLAND, SYDNEY HARRIS, GEORGE RICHARDS.

The Committee of the NATIONAL SCHOOLS are thankful to be able to present so prosperous a statement of their funds.

During the past year, the Ladies' Committee of the Girls' School requested that the whole affairs of the School should be managed by one Committee, to which the gentlemen acceded, and the whole National School, boys and girls, is now under the management of the gentlemen who are responsible for the expenses of the Schools; and as they had lost the generous assistance of one member, who had been removed by death, they were obliged to canvass the town, and several new subscribers were obtained.

The Committee have been at considerable expense in repairing the premises, and they are now in good tenantable repair.

The number of boys, at present on the books, is 180, with an average attendance of 130; and of girls 107, with an average of 65.

They have engaged a Certificated Mistress, and they have every reason to believe that the girls will, at the Inspector's visit this year, present as good a report as the boys' school has of late.

The Government Inspector's report, last year, was:—

" BOYS.—This School improves every year. The boys answer with much intelligence. All the work is carefully done. The Writing is clear and bold throughout the School; the Arithmetic good, and the Grammar uncommonly good."

" GIRLS.—This School is much as in former years; the children are lively and bright, but know very little. I am glad to find that a Certificated Teacher is about to be appointed, and that the promoters are determined to make the School thoroughly efficient."

Your Committee feel satisfied that the discipline and religious instruction given in our Schools are most likely to train up the young in habits of virtue and morality; and make them " honor all men; fear God; and honor the Queen;" and therefore they confidently appeal to their fellow-townsmen for a continuance of their support.

The affairs of both the Boys' National and the Girls' National (St James') were now managed by one Committee.

From the appended Poole National Schools Report for 1861, it will be noted that the number of boys on the roll at that time was 180 and the girls, 107.

St James' (Poole Boys' National School)

The Register of St James Church began in 1558, and in 1789 a Sunday School was started, By 1821 numbers attending had swollen to the extent that two day classes were in operation, one in the tower of the newly built parish church, and another in the room adjoining the church. There were 114 boys and 95 girls in attendance at that time.

In 1835 the boys moved to their new **National School** at Perry Gardens, and the **Poole Girls' National School** opened opposite St James Church in Church Street in 1863.

Poole Boys' National School was built by Henry Knight and opened in 1835. It was funded by £100 contribution from the Corporation, £150 from the National Society, and the remainder from private subscriptions aided by the proceeds of Harbin's Charity. This Charity was set up according to the Will of Mr. Henry Harbin, a London merchant, who was Mayor of Poole in 1642, and elected a free burgess in 1701. The National was situated at what was then the top of Lagland Street, called Perry Gardens, the site is now occupied by a block of flats (opposite Poole Advice Centre - which was originally the Labour Exchange and later, as Portcullis House, used by the Customs & Excise).

The first Log Book available is dated 1878 when the Headmaster was Thomas Laws, who was assisted by W. H. Knight, who had been a pupil at the National School until the age of 14 years when he straightaway became a master, and in 1910 became a School Attendance Officer.

Thomas Laws had taken over the Headmastership from a William Drew, and he seemed to put great stress on the boys preparing for the annual inspection, which at this time was carried out by a Reverend Wm. Tregarthen, H.M. Inspector of Schools. But alas Reverend Tregarthen had this to say: *"The general efficiency of the school is very fair but the lower standards require increased attention, their work is poor"*. However, a year later Mr Laws' dedication was repaid when the Inspectors reported that *"The Boys' School has passed a very creditable examination. There has been most satisfactory improvement during the past year"*.

Attendance round about the 1880's fluctuated between 175 and 185 pupils, and it is interesting to note that such local events as the Band of Hope Fete and Sangers' Circus could make a drop in the school attendance.

As this was a National School, religious instruction was given great emphasis. The Old Testament, the New Testament, the Prayer Book, Litany,

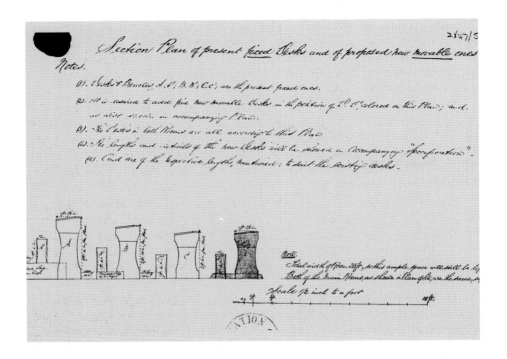

Section Plan of present fixed Desks and of proposed new movable ones

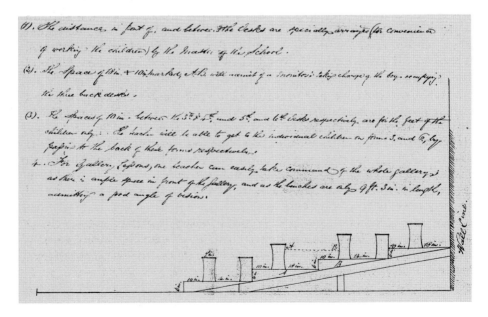

Plans to replace existing fixed desks with movable ones to accommodate increasing numbers of pupils.

Catechism and the Lord's Prayer all had to be thoroughly learnt in preparation for a special Inspector's report. Remembering how very poor most of the lads attending this school must have been, the syllabus was wide and varied, ranging from reading, writing, arithmetic, spelling, mental arithmetic, English, recitation, geography, singing and book-keeping.

Even in those days new schools soon outgrew themselves, for in 1883 Thomas Laws writes, *"Unsatisfactory classroom reported last year not yet been enlarged"*. The wheels of officialdom ground slowly for it was not until 1898 that the new classroom was built. Very detailed specifications of the plans of the existing desks and the proposed new benches and gallery for the new classroom, are appended.

Around this time epidemics of measles were sufficient grounds for the Medical Officer of Health to order the closure of the school, and apart from the ordinary attendance register, an epidemic register was also required to be kept. Truancy was no stranger to this school, and the Headmaster states in his log in 1898 – *"The discipline of the school suffers owing to the talkative tendency during school hours"*.

In August of 1900, J. P. Coningham (of London) commenced his duties as Headmaster. Poole, by 1900, had a beautiful public Free Library and School of Art situated very close to the National School, at the top of Mount Street. It had been erected in 1887 by J. J. Norton to commemorate the Queen's Golden Jubilee, and the cost is reported to have been £2,500. Poole Park, with its beautiful Lake and Bandstand, had been opened in 1890 on ground which had been donated to the town by Lady Wimborne, plus the addition of some adjoining land purchased by Poole Council. By this time two other schools had opened in close proximity to the National School; the National School No.2 Infants' (St Paul's) Perry Gardens, and the Lagland Street School run by Miss Rattray.

At the beginning of the twentieth century, all registered fishing boats and implements belonging to the Port of Poole were required to be distinguished by the addition of the letters PE, and the Poole Borough Police in Market Street sported one Superintendent, two Sergeants and ten Constables. The Railway Time Table was printed, but back at school work was still chalked on slates. Oil lamps lit the schoolrooms, and heating was supplied by coal fires. Transport would still for the most part have been by horse and cart, and maybe penny-farthing bicycles.

The year 1901 saw the death of Queen Victoria and the proclamation of Edward VII as King. In May of 1901 a dispirited Mr Coningham wrote – *"Now the fine weather is coming on, the boys are starting their old system of half-days, truanting is still prevalent, having caned six this week. The attendance barely reached 90"*.

In July it was still hot, mumps were prevalent and he writes in his log book for July 12th – *"Boys hot and lazy and dirty"*. However by March of 1902, the new Headmaster seems to have made his mark, for the report by H.M. Inspector says *"The Boys' School now takes a higher position than in any*

1899 National Infants Group 3, with Teacher.

previous year for tone, discipline and attainment. The written word is well carried out and interest shown. Singing deserves praise". Signed - Archibald H. Yeatman.

Empire Day and Trafalgar Day were always well remembered, and 21st October 1903 was no exception. Reverend John Archibald Lawson visited and gave a discourse from 4.00 p.m. to 4.30 p.m. on "Duty", emphasising the same from the character of Nelson. The very great interest that Reverend A. Lawson had in all things nautical ensured that Trafalgar Day was always well commemorated in Poole Schools. It was on this day of 1897 that the Mariners' Window (East) of St James' was unveiled.

His death in September 1905 at 72 years of age caused widespread grief throughout the town, for "Daddy" Lawson was beloved by all. His keen involvement in the British and Foreign Bible Society had brought him into close contact with the Nonconformist Ministers of the town, and so also, indirectly, with their congregations. To mourn his passing the flags on St James' tower and all public buildings were flown at half-mast and the bells tolled. Shops and private residents alike paid last respects by the erection of black shutters and drawn blinds. Nearly the total populace of Poole turned out to pay their last respects to the funeral procession by standing silently, the ladies maybe weeping and the men doffing their hats or caps as the cortege passed. It is significant that Mr J. P. Coningham, Head of the National School, read the lessons at the Memorial Service.

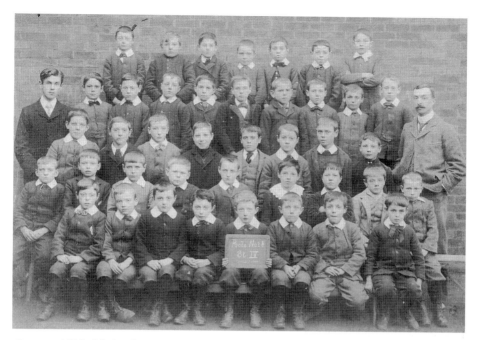

January 1902, National Boys' Standard IV with Mr Knight, Headmaster, on right and Mr Maunder standing left.

Poole appears to have had its share of snow even in the "good old days", and 1908 was no exception. Because of the hard winter butchers in the High Street gave meat to make soup which was distributed from the Guildhall steps in Market Street and from the Soup Kitchen run at 145 Lagland Street, a house just below the School (next to Whitty's Coal Yard).

Slate gave way to pen and paper by the time the next Headmaster, Mr A. J. Martin, took up his headship in 1910 from an ailing Mr Coningham. This same year, on 5th September Mr H. P. Smith commenced duties there as an uncertificated teacher at £65 p.a.

There was really close liaison between the Boys' National on the one side of Lagland Street and the **No. 2 Infants' School (St Paul's)** almost directly opposite on the corner of Globe Lane, whose first Head was Miss F. M. Golledge. These two schools, together with St James' Girls' School, were frequently visited by the clergy of St James and St Paul's, and religious instruction given.

Early in 1911, a census took place in Poole and once again measles reared its ugly head. Not only did it affect attendance at the National, but the Infants' school had to close down because of the epidemic. Later, in June of that year both schools were closed from the 19th to 23rd for the Coronation celebrations of King George V. On the 27th June, the Mayor, Alderman

Leonard D. Ballard, visited the school and distributed to every boy present a fancy box of chocolates as a Coronation memento. During this time, the measles' epidemic continued to spread, and the National School was forced to close in July.

By September school lessons were in full swing again, and lectures on Alcohol were given by Mr Archer Reed from the Western Temperance League. On the lighter side, a lantern lecture on New Zealand was held in the presence of 200 boys. At Christmas time the lads of the school were well treated by some of the wealthier citizens of the town, and events such as a visit to tea and a concert arranged by the Bournemouth Scouts, 16th Troop, took place.

It was also in 1911 that construction commenced of the nearby new School at South Road, providing accommodation for 600 children. This school was to be opened in 1912 but the work at the National School continued undaunted and a really new project which aroused a great deal of local interest was "the School Garden". It even became the substance of several newspaper articles. No less a person than the Mayor of Poole, together with the Borough Surveyor, was responsible in conjunction with the Head Master (Mr Martin) for acquiring the use of a piece of land situated in the Ladies' Walking Field behind the old White House Laundry. Some may recall that the laundry was adjacent to the main railway line near the public footbridge which still stands in the High Street. It would appear that the Council were obviously impressed with this project, for it is recorded that on the 16th April 1912 they allowed the sum of £3 for expenses and practical gardening classes commenced on a regular basis. Enthusiasm knew no bounds for on the 19th July Councillor H. Saunders kindly gave a load of manure for the school garden. On one evening 50 parents visited the garden to view the progress made by the boys from the "National".

When the school reopened after the Summer holidays on August 26th a great deal of concern was caused over an act of vandalism committed by two lads who forced an entry into the school during the holidays. The locks of four cupboards were wrenched open by means of a poker and the contents strewn over the floor and considerable damage had also been created. The Standard One Register for 1911-12 was terribly marked and painted with red ink. The two lads responsible were caught by a policeman in the cloakroom. On Thursday August 15th, they were summoned by the Managers and were fined 5/- each for damages and 5/- each for costs.

At the beginning of 1913 the school was visited by H.M. Inspectors who subsequently reported very favourably on the standard of teaching and the general improvement in the work produced by the pupils, but there was adverse comment in respect of premises and equipment. The Inspectors were of the opinion that the cloakroom did not provide sufficient accommodation for the clothes of all the boys and they considered it undesirable that the boys should continue to carry their caps into school. The classrooms in winter were heated by oil stoves, which were unprotected by guards and proved quite

Some of the names of the infants recalled about 1906.
Murray, Rowe, Fisher, H Burt, Shiner (brother and sister), F Murray, Hilda Greenhill,
F Dyke, Fred Jeans, Reg Elkins, D Faulkner, N Knobbs, E Mitchell, D Cartridge,
D Greenslade, E Cave, Gladys Balson, Vera Whittaker, Fred Balson, Reed,
Brown and Cartridges.
Miss Hughes (not in the photo) was headmistress at the time.

inadequate. The gas lights were often lit in order to provide a little additional heat.

It was unfortunate that Poole had more than its fair share of rain during the year and gardening lessons were continually cancelled. Perhaps the disappointment suffered in this connection was more than compensated for when the National School lads won the Tug of War Shield at the Shop Assistants' Carnival and Sports Day held in September. The 8 lads responsible for this achievement each received a medal and no doubt were very proud of their triumph. The excitement of this event appears to have been short lived, for it was about this time that the facilities at the school once again became the subject of much criticism, arising from the visit of the Medical Officer of Health for Poole and the Sanitary Inspectors. The latrines situated at the back of the school were the subject of attack and the cloakrooms and heating were greeted with similar disapproval as reported by H.M. Inspectors.

Empire Day was a significant event and patriotic songs were always sung in the morning of May 23rd. This was followed by a half-day holiday in the afternoon. Unthinkable as it would be these days, it is recorded that 20 lads dressed as "nigger boys" entered the Poole Shop Assistants' Carnival in June 1914 and won the second prize. July was not such a happy month. Five lads suffering from consumption were taken off the books and the Great War loomed. One of the teachers, Mr W. J. Robbins, volunteered for the Forces and was accepted for Lord Kitchener's Army. Another teacher, Mrs J. L. Crowe, was granted an afternoon absence to see her husband depart for India with the 7th Hants Territorial Forces.

Evidence of the war soon became apparent, for on 18th November 1914 the National lads were marched to Station Road to witness the military funeral procession of a Belgian soldier. Whether out of patriotism, excitement or merely in search of adventure, many of the lads themselves left school and managed to join the Forces, including my father, Arthur John, "Jack" Blundell. Despite the great poverty surrounding the lads that were left, they did their bit and the war effort was well supported from the National School. In December 1916 the sum of 12s.7d. was sent to the organisers of the Overseas Club, which provided tobacco and comforts for the troops and this was followed in April 1917 by a donation of £1 to the RSPCA towards the cost of medical care for sick and wounded horses at the front.

Poole suffered severe cold weather and snow storms in the early months of 1917 and one wonders if the disappearance of the wooden lavatory seats on 12th January had root cause in someone needing firewood. September was a brighter month for the teachers as they were awarded a general salary increase. Head Masters received a maximum of £270 per annum and Head Mistresses of schools with more that 100 pupils a maximum of £175. Mr Martin was granted exemption from military service by the local Tribunal for so long as he remained Head of the National School and on the further understanding that he joined a volunteer training course. This decision was later contested by the National Services Representative but having fulfilled the conditions, Mr Martin stayed on at the school and was to become a staunch member of the Volunteer Training Corps for the next 40 years.

At the beginning of 1918, members of the staff gave their services for Food Control work at the Town Hall and the lads were beseeched to collect fruit stones, as these, it is recorded, were used in the manufacture of gas masks. Peace dawned and the Armistice was signed on the 11th November. It was not long before mundane matters once more ruled with influenza and scabies being rampant.

As there is very little on record for the year 1919, one can only assume that the school, in keeping with the town in general, was experiencing a period of post-war adjustment. It is noticeable however, that on various days in July the school was closed by order of the local Education Authority. One occasion being the 18th July when the children were taken to Poole Park for tea and sports as part of the Peace celebrations.

Everything appears to have run smoothly until the early part of 1920, where a great deal of aggravation was experienced with the urinals. On 12th January, Boones (who are still trading in Poole High Street) were requested to replace the padlocks for the gates. Presumably this was to stop young vandals from entering after school hours. In addition to the urinal problem, an influenza epidemic once again took its toll during January and February.

In June – in addition to the normal Whitsun holidays – a half day holiday was also granted on the occasion of the Congregational Sunday School treat. On 11th June, 169 boys with 107 girls of St James' School, 50 parents, Reverend H. L. Phillips, and Alderman Ballard and the staff of both schools journeyed in motor buses to Milford-on-Sea. No doubt a very exciting day out, and probably the farthest from home that some of the children had travelled. One can imagine those parents left at home congregating later in the day anxiously awaiting the return of their little ones. The school closed for the summer holiday towards the end of July, and re-opened on 22nd August. During the vacation the school was completely redecorated throughout by Mr Foot. New stoves had been provided and a new grate replaced the old one in the small classroom.

As all the normal activities continued to flourish, so did the school garden. In fact the weather was so favourable for seed sowing that on 10th March 1921 the school timetable was altered to provide for extra gardening lessons. Empire Day and all royal occasions still took a prominent place in the school life, and 1923 was no exception for in accordance with the King's wish the school was closed on 26th April to celebrate the Duke of York's wedding day. Moving to the end of the year, the log dated 21st December is worthy of note, for one can sense that the entry was made in true Christmas spirit. It is written – *"School closed after the morning session for the Christmas holidays. At 4 p. m. the boys assembled for a Christmas party, tea was provided by Mr Thacker of Westbourne, who also gave every lad an orange and some sweets. Toys and books for each lad were given by the British Broadcasting Company, and distributed to the boys by Mrs Herring of Princes Road, Westbourne. A wireless concert was given through the kindness of Mr Jock Crockett, and Mrs Lewis entertained the children with stories and recitations."*

An important national event in 1924 was the British Empire Exhibition held at Wembley in July of that year. Forty-one lads accepted the opportunity of a day out to view the Exhibition. They were accompanied by the Headmaster together with Messrs Trimm and Matthews. The Reverend H. L. Phillips, having resigned the living of St James, visited the school on 27th October to say goodbye to the scholars and staff. As was to become the custom, Armistice Day was celebrated on 11th November and the lads, standing in their places, observed two minutes silence. Talks were given throughout the school on the significance of Armistice Day.

On 15th July 1925, the Schools' Sports Day was held in Poole Park and for the occasion the school was granted a holiday. The rowing team – Shannon, A. Wills and L. Wills – won the Rowing Shield and medals. The tug-of-war team also did well to reach the finals but unfortunately lost by two pulls to one. The winter months were clouded by the death of Queen Alexandra who was duly mourned by the rendering of the Dead March whilst the lads stood to attention on 27th November 1925.

It became traditional for the lads to attend the service in St Paul's church on Ash Wednesday and the 17th February 1926 was no exception. The school closed for its annual outing on 2nd July. About 130 lads accompanied by the teachers, the girls from St James' School and about 50 parents journeyed to Lulworth Cove by charabanc. The Reverend C.E. and Mrs Williams also motored to Lulworth during the day in order to put in an appearance. Joseph Burden of Standard II met with an accident running a splinter into his buttocks. The young lad was transported by motorcar to the Cornelia Hospital at Poole. Events indicate that the autumn of this year proved very wet for it is recorded on 22nd October that attendance had dropped very considerably owing to the excessively wet weather. Furthermore the desks in Standard IV had to be moved owing to leaks in the roof. This of course was reported to the authorities. It was also necessary to advise Mr Rueben White the owner of the adjoining property that the water from his roof was running into the school playgrounds. With the advent of the Christmas festivities, some 30 of the poorest boys were taken to a party at the Canford Cliffs village hall on 20th December, and on the 23rd of the month the school was closed in the morning for the Christmas holiday, but before leaving, fruit, sweets and toys were distributed to each of the lads.

On the occasion of a Royal visit in the month of October 1927, the lads were assembled at an allotted place in the Park to witness the Prince of Wales place a wreath at the foot of the War Memorial. In November 100 lads were taken to the newly opened Regent Cinema, which once stood on the site now occupied by Boots in the Dolphin Centre. The object of the visit was to see a film in connection with the League of Nations. On another occasion 80 lads attended to see a film about the British Empire.

During the early months of 1928 considerable pleasure was experienced from the favourable reports received. In March the Diocesan Inspector of Schools had this to say *"This school in its religious instruction is doing work that is distinctive in quality and of very great religious value. It is characterised by the thoroughness of its planning, the definiteness of its aim and the thoroughness of its execution"*. On 4th May, HM Inspectors reported *"The excellent tone of the school is again a striking feature. The boys are delightfully keen and responsive and receive a thorough training in habits of industry and application"*.

As reference has already been made to the Regent Theatre, it is worth noting that 17 lads accompanied by the Head Master visited the theatre on the 23rd May for the ceremony of the Town Council conferring the Freedom of the Borough on Alderman Herbert S. Carter, JP.

By 1930, plans for a remodelled building were being considered. The fresh water supply had been connected to the latrines in place of salt water which had previously been used. The fresh water supply was also used to serve a drinking fountain recently installed in the play ground. With the opening of new open air swimming baths in Park Lake Road, bathing lessons were commenced and took place every Friday at 3.30 p.m. with Mr Sharpe in charge. This class was for 30 lads and later another 20 were allowed to attend on Wednesday mornings. This swimming bath has now been demolished and replaced by the very modern indoor swimming pool in Kingland Road

1931 saw the introduction of school milk available in 1/3 pint cartons for

1935 Boys' National Reunion Committee.
Centre: Seated row Mr A J Martin (Headmaster), with the Reverand R. Farthing on his right.
Other names recalled, I Davis, E Mitchell, Milledge, R Hurst, F Froud, Stickland.

boys who could pay one penny each morning at 10.30 a.m. The milk was supplied by the Bladen Dairies and about 144 boys took advantage of this nourishment.

Extensive repairs and renewals were carried out throughout this school in 1932. A new stove was placed in No. 2 room and a new fire grate in the big class room. The gas pipes were replaced and new lamps installed. Repairs to the roof took place and the playground received attention with the gravelled part being asphalted. The railings were put in good order and of course the urinals were seen to once again and whitewashed.

No sooner was the school looking as bright and clean as it ever had, when at the weekend of Saturday, 24th September 1932, three lads – aged 8, 7 and 4 – entered the school through a window causing considerable damage. The next day, Sunday, the Rector, Reverend B. Herklots, the Vicar, Reverend R. Farthing, the Mayor, H. S. Carter, Major Wheatley and many councillors visited to view the damage that had taken place. No school could be held on the Monday and a squad of boys aided the staff to sort everything out. Extra help was engaged to assist the Caretakers scrub the school throughout. Acting on instructions from the Chairman and Vice Chairman of the local Education Authority, two of the boys were publicly caned by the Head Master on the 28th September.

In November of that year the Cenotaph Service from Whitehall was for the first time relayed to some of the boys through the medium of a wireless set loaned by Mr Francis.

In early 1933 the National School received a grant from the Town Council to purchase a wireless set for their use. Corporation workmen erected two wireless aerial poles and on the 2nd March 1933 a wireless licence was purchased. So many boys were now coming to school by cycle that it was deemed necessary during the Whitsun holidays to erect a cycle shed to accommodate them.

Towards the end of the year the necessitous children ceased to be supplied with free milk and biscuits. These children were supplied instead with tickets to obtain a free midday meal from the soup kitchen. Within a year free issue of milk had commenced again together with biscuits and cod liver oil and malt. During 1934 preparations were discussed in connection with the Centenary Celebrations of the National School.

The Round Tablers invited 35 of the boys to a party at the Guildhall, some 50 boys rendered sea shanties at the old Conference Hall. At school the boys received lectures on the care of their teeth and RSPCA work. Two telephones from the Town Clerk's Office were installed at school and the boys of the Carpentry Class had really made strides in assembling hurdles, jumping stands and a swimming frame for their use. Just before the boys broke up for the Christmas recess, Councillor Stickland -himself an old boy of the National - visited the school and presented every boy with a stick of Poole rock.

The centenary of the National School was celebrated in 1935 and on 24th February there was a mammoth church parade attended by approximately 400 old scholars, in addition to the present scholars. Leading the parade was the Poole Town Band. Together they marched to St James Church for a centenary service, during which the lessons were read by Councillor W. J. Stickland, an old boy, and Mr A. E. Goff, a Manager. The sermon was preached by Rev. R. Farthing, Vicar of St Paul's, which used to stand in the High Street opposite Globe Lane. In Poole Park a wreath in memory of the old boys who fell in the Great War was laid at the foot of the War Memorial by Sgt. H. Knight, VC, an old boy of the school. On the 28th February an Old Boys' Reunion Dinner was held in the Centenary Hall, Wimborne Road, which again was well attended by some 400 old pupils.

The Silver Jubilee of King George V and Queen Mary took place in May and as part of the Jubilee Festival boys journeyed to the Park in procession with other schools and at the conclusion of formalities, tea was provided. Every child present received a Jubilee aluminium beaker embossed with the heads of the King and Queen and the date. At the request of the King, a holiday was granted on the 6th November, for it was on this day that the wedding took place of the Duke of Gloucester and Princess Alice.

The health of King George V was gradually deteriorating and his death was announced on the 21st January 1936. The following day Edward VIII was proclaimed King. The school assembled at 10 a.m. and the National Anthem was sung at the end of the royal proclamation. The funeral of King George V took place six days later.

Time was running out at the National School and after having been an elementary school since 1835, it eventually closed in 1939. Some 60 lads were transferred to Henry Harbin Secondary Modern School and 126 lads moved to the South Road Junior School. Teachers Francis, Sharp and Flatt were assigned to Henry Harbin and teachers Martin, Beale and Evans transferred to South Road School.

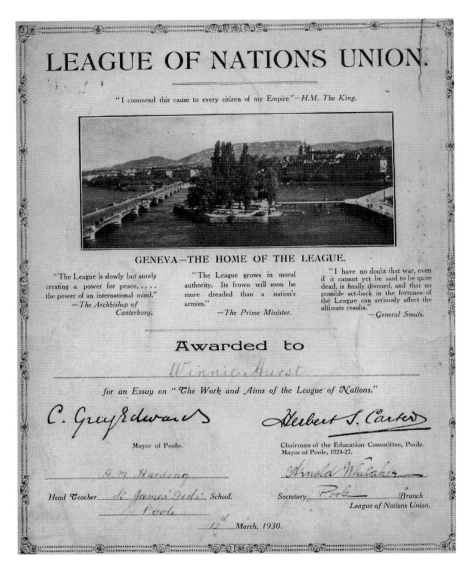

League of Nations Union Certificate.
March 1930
Awarded to head girl, Winnie Hurst for her essay on the Work and Aims of the League of Nations. She was an exemplary pupil who, unusually in those days, remained at school until she was past fifteen years of age.

St James' Girls' Section
(Poole Girls' National School)

Following the transfer in 1835 of the Boys' Section of St. James' to the new National School in Perry Gardens, the Girls and Infants were able to take advantage of the extra space by occupying the two classrooms at St. James' previously used by the Boys, where they remained until the new classroom was opened opposite the church in Church Street during the year 1863. The dimensions of this new classroom were a great improvement on the old, being 34' long, 18' 6" wide and 17' high.

Many changes had taken place in England since the departure of the boys to Perry Gardens. Queen Victoria was by now firmly established on the throne and in the 1840's the force of evangelical religion had started to take effect. It also became obligatory to register all births and deaths. The latter half of the nineteenth century saw a considerable increase in the population of the country and people became more aware of themselves and the environment. Possibly some of the changes were attributable to the Industrial Revolution of earlier years. The Coalmines Act of 1842 prohibited the employment underground of women and all children under 10 years of age. Further protective legislation was introduced with the Factory Act of 1844, which enforced the fencing of machinery and also stipulated that women should work no longer than 12 hours per day and children under 13 years of age not more than 6½ hours per day. This Act was soon to be superseded by the Factory Act of 1847, which enforced a maximum of 10 hours' work per day for women. It was around this time that the country also experienced a period of free trade, although the Corn Laws continued to be the subject of political issues. In 1847 the powers conferred upon the Poor Law Commissioners were transferred to a Board under the charge of a minister and in the ensuing year, the Public Health Act 1848 made local Boards of Health responsible for the well being of the people. Regulations for the closure of schools and exclusion of children from school suffering certain specified complaints were very properly defined. The various types of illness provided for under these regulations included scarlet fever, diphtheria, smallpox, erysipelas, typhoid and the typhus fevers, measles, whooping cough, mumps, chicken pox, parasitic diseases which included ringworm or itch and verminous conditions, impetigo and consumption.

The opening in 1863 of the new classroom in Church Street was unfortunately marred by an epidemic of scarlet fever, but after a three week holiday in August, the school returned to normal and the girls' new Head Mistress, Henrietta Clarke, commenced her duties. There were 78 children registered at the school and on the 2nd September Laura Goff was appointed Monitor for the Infants class (Division 2). The parents witnessed the decline of the Newfoundland shipping trade from the Quay, which was attributable to the inability of the merchants of Poole to compete with large vessels from ports such as Liverpool and Glasgow. The harbour was, however, rich with fish, especially plaice, and oyster beds were already a feature. Potteries had started to develop in close vicinity of the Quay and local clay was being shipped to Staffordshire. Cordage, netting, sail cloths and all shipping requisites were produced in abundance and some of the fastest yachts were built in Poole. Corn and flour trades flourished on the Quay and an architectural pottery company (with offices in London) became established near the railway station at Hamworthy. The iron foundry of Lewin and Wilkinson also set seal on what was to become a very important local industry.

Under the parliamentary electoral system of the day, Poole was entitled to two Members of Parliament. High Street boasted 2 hatters and 2 pawnbrokers and within two minutes' walk of the Quay there were 38 taverns or public houses, many of which are still in use today and bearing the same name as then. The foremost of these is, of course, the Antelope Hotel standing at the lower end of High Street, which also had been the daily departure point for coaches to London, Bath and Bristol. A subsequent service of conveyances operated at frequent intervals from the London Hotel in High Street to the railway station and Poole Junction to co-incide with the arrival and departure of trains and goods. Also of significance around this period was the granting of a regular water supply to the town. Market Street was locally renowned for the markets held on Monday and Thursday of each week. The Saints days of 1st May (St Philip & St James) and 1st November (All Saints) attracted two town fairs. These were great occasions of importance to the townsfolk and the children were likewise affected. Inevitably school attendances dropped on special occasions, sometimes to the extent that a holiday was granted.

Most of the girls attending school in Church Street in those early days came from working class families, who lived frugally in the terraced houses within local proximity. The front doors of these houses opened directly onto the pavements and often the backyards were communal with perhaps a water pump and trough and one lavatory complete with a boarded seat like a throne and a pull chain. These facilities were shared between as many as five houses and such conditions were not conducive to cleanliness. Miss Clarke, Head Mistress of St. James' Girls, was obliged on various occasions to send home several girls suffering with the "itch". In fact, on 14th September 1863, Miss Clarke refused to admit two girls for the very same reason and on the following day another girl was sent home and told to remain there until she recovered from the itch. This particular girl's mother took offence and sent her daughter to a private school! Whatever the problems, it would seem that the scripture lessons were always continued and also the girls were encouraged to become good needlewomen. Maybe the fact that some of the poor children

REVISED EDITION.
By order of the Education Committee.

BOROUGH OF POOLE.

REGULATIONS FOR CLOSURE
OF AND
EXCLUSION OF CHILDREN FROM SCHOOL.

PART I.—SCHOOL CLOSURE.

MANAGERS.

1. If the Sanitary Authority requires the Closure in accordance with Article 57 of the Code, the order must be at once complied with by the Managers.

2. The Managers should at once comply with a Certificate recommending closure from the Medical Officer of Health.

3. If the Managers desire advice or authority as to closure, they should apply for the authority of the School Medical Officer, under Article 45 (b), on the form prescribed.

PART II.—EXCLUSION.

MANAGERS.

4. For the purposes of the Code it shall be deemed to be exclusion on reasonable grounds when individual children are excluded from School on either of the grounds mentioned in Article 53 (b), (1), (2), (3), provided (1), that the School Medical Officer has authorised their exclusion under Article 53 (b) or (ii), that the Sanitary Authority has required their exclusion under Article 57.

5. When an order is issued by the Sanitary Authority that certain children are to be excluded, or if the Medical Officer of Health certify that their exclusion is necessary, the order or certificate must be at once complied with.

6. In every case when a child has been excluded from School, or when it is desired to exclude a child from School, information must be at once sent to the School Medical Officer. The name, address, and ground for exclusion should be given in every case.

7. The Managers shall give reasonable facilities to the School Medical Officer, so far as lies in their power, to enable him to ascertain and certify cases in which the exclusion of children from School is desirable.

8. Managers and Head Teachers should exclude cases and suspected cases of infectious disease, and children who have recently been in contact with such cases, and children with parasitic diseases, and they may exclude uncleanly or verminous children, without first referring the matter to the School Medical Officer, but they must immediately send a notification of such exclusion, accompanied by full particulars, so that the necessary certificate may be issued by the School Medical Officer.

9. Every Certificate given by the School Medical Officer must be carefully preserved and must be produced, if required, to any Inspector or Officer of the Board of Education's Medical Department.

---

10. The School Medical Officer shall reserve the right to refuse a Certificate when he is not satisfied as to the information given.

HEAD TEACHER (*See Regulation 8 also*).

11. When an order is issued by the Sanitary Authority that certain children are to be excluded, or if the Medical Officer of Health request their exclusion in writing, the order or request must be at once complied with.

12. In every case when a child has been excluded from School for any reason, or when it is desired to exclude a child from School, information must be at once sent to the School Medical Officer for his formal authorisation. The name, address, and grounds for exclusion must be given in every case.

13. The Head Teacher shall, on the outbreak of an infectious disease in the School or place in which it is situated, issue such warning notices to parents as the Education Committee may direct on the advice of the School Medical Officer.

14. The Head Teacher shall send immediate information of every case of infectious disease (both notifiable and non-notifiable), and of every suspected case occurring among the scholars, to the School Medical Officer.

15. Every child suffering, or suspected to be suffering, or suspected of recently having suffered, from any infectious or contagious disease must be at once excluded from School. Suspected cases should not be re-admitted until a *certificate of freedom* from infectious or contageous disease has been produced.

16. Every child coming from a house in which there is a case of infectious disease must be excluded from School. (For exceptions to this rule see under "Measles," "Whooping-Cough," "Chicken-Pox," and "Mumps." *If however, the Managers desire to exclude all children from infected houses they may do so.*)

---

17. When a case of infectious disease has already occurred in a School, a careful watch should be kept for children with suspicious symptons, and they must be at once excluded.

18. A child who has been in a Hospital for Infectious Diseases must not return to the School for at least a fortnight after discharge from Hospital.

PROCEDURE.

The following is the detailed procedure to be followed with regard to the different diseases :—

SCARLET FEVER.

The Sick Child or children to be excluded at least **8 weeks.** Before re-admission, permission must be obtained in writing from the Medical Officer of Health.

Children from the same house are to be excluded for **14 days** after the date of the removal of the sick child to Hospital, and until permission has been obtained in writing from the Medical Officer of Health.

If the sick child is kept at home, the other children can be excluded during the **whole time** the child is ill, and for 14 days in addition after the date the child has been pronounced free from infection.

Suspicious Cases.—Any child in the School who has a headache, or vomiting, or fever, or sore throat, or rash, or whose hands or neck shew signs of peeling, should be excluded. **If one or more known cases of the diseases have occurred,** a single one of these symptoms in a child justifies its exclusion. The exclusion should be for one week, but no child who has had a sore throat, or rash, or peeling, should be re-admitted until it has been seen by the School Medical Officer and given a certificate to return to School.

---

8 pages of 'EXCLUSIONS' on Medical Grounds,
continued overleaf.

5

DIPHTHERIA.

The Sick Child to be excluded until a certificate from the Medical Officer of Health states the child is free of infection. This certificate will be based on Bacteriological evidence.

Children from the same house are to be excluded for 14 days after the removal of sick child to Hospital, and until permission has been obtained in writing from the Medical Officer of Health.

If the sick child is kept at home, the other children must be excluded during the whole time the child is infectious, and for 14 days in addition after the date the child is pronounced, free from infection.

Suspicious Cases.—Any child in the School who has a sore throat, or headache, or vomiting, should also be excluded, provided that a known case of the disease has occurred. The exclusion should be for one week, but no child who has had a sore throat should be re-admitted unless *certified free* from disease.

SMALL-POX, ERYSIPELAS, TYPHOID and TYPHUS FEVERS.

Sick children must be excluded until *certified free* from infection by the Medical Officer of Health.

Children coming from houses where Erysipelas or Typhoid Fever exists, but who are not themselves suffering from the disease, should not be excluded from School.

Children coming from houses where cases of Small-Pox or Typhus Fever have occurred should be excluded for three weeks after removal of the case and disinfection of the house.

MEASLES.

The sick child to be excluded for at least 3 weeks.

Children from the same house to be excluded for 14 days from date on which child is taken ill. (See exception below).

6

If fresh cases occur in the house, children attending an Infants School or class, must be excluded longer, so that 14 days elapse after occurrence of last case. The period need not be extended in case of children attending other schools or classes.

Suspicious Cases.—If cases have occurred, exclude children with watering eyes, colds in head, or rash on the face.

Exception.—Children who have already had the disease and are not attending an Infants school or class, need not be excluded at all from School.

WHOOPING-COUGH.

The sick child to be excluded at least 6 weeks, and not to be re-admitted then if there are still paroxysms of coughing.

Children from the same house to be excluded for 18 days from the date on which the child is taken ill.—(See exception). .

Suspicious Cases.—If a case has occurred, any children who have severe attacks of coughing, especially if followed by sickness, should be excluded. The characteristic " whoop ", may not occur for from 10 days to 3 weeks after the cough begins, although the child is meanwhile infectious.

Exception.—Children who have already had the disease and are not attending an Infants School or class, need not be excluded at all from School.

MUMPS.

The sick child to be excluded for three weeks.

Children from the same house to be excluded for two weeks unless they have already had the disease.

Suspicious Cases.—Exclude children with tenderness and swelling in front of ears and behind jaws.

7

CHICKEN POX.

The sick child to be excluded at least three weeks, and until every scab has fallen off the body.

Children from the same house to be excluded for 14 days, unless they have already had the disease.

Suspicious Cases.—Children with red spots on the face or chest which become like small blisters should also be excluded.

PARASITIC DISEASES.

All children suffering or suspected to be suffering from Ringworm or Itch must be immediately excluded from School, and must not be allowed to return *until certified* by the School Medical Officer to be free from the disease.

VERMINOUS CONDITIONS.

All children in whose heads or on whose bodies or clothes lice are actually seen, should be excluded from School until free from them. A child need not be excluded if " nits " only are present in the hair, unless these are present in large numbers, or the parents are making no effectual efforts to get rid of them. The exclusion should be until a certain date, a reasonable time (a week) being allowed for cleansing.

The Managers may, at their discretion, demand a *satisfactory certificate of freedom* from verminous conditions as a condition of re-admission.

If the child does not return to School on the date fixed with a satisfactory certificate of freedom from verminous conditions, the Managers are to report the case to the Local Attendance Committee.

The Local Attendance Committee, if they decide to institute proceedings, are to refer the matter to the Secretary of Education, so that they may have legal assistance.

All children with unclean heads should be reported to the Medical Officer, when instructions for cleansing will be sent to the parents.

8

IMPETIGO.

This is an infectious form of eczema. It usually occurs on the face and hands in the form of yellowish brown, raised scabs. Children who have it must be excluded until the scabs have disappeared.

TUBERCLE OF LUNG (PHTHISIS, OR CONSUMPTION).

A child with this disease is to be excluded.

SCHOOL ATTENDANCE OFFICER.

19. The School Attendance Officer shall at once inform the Medical Officer of Health and the Head Teacher of any children whom he may suspect of suffering from, or of recently having suffered from, an infectious or contagious disease, and the latter shall forthwith exclude the same.

20. The School Attendance Officer shall report to the Medical Officer of Health where several children in the same family are absent from School.

21. The homes of children absent from School on account of disease to be visited at least once monthly, and a report to be sent to the Medical Officer, when a doctor is not in attendance.

The School Medical Officer attends at the Municipal Offices, Market Street, Poole, at 10 a.m. each morning, and at Branksome Council Offices, Library Road, every Tuesday at 2-30 p.m., to examine children unable to attend School, to give certificates of exclusion or re-admission after illness, and to undertake the treatment of minor ailments in School children.

had their clothes sewn on to them had something to do with the tuition. Punishment was always at hand for on the 26th January 1864, the needlework produced by two of the girls was so bad that the teacher was obliged to punish them. No details are available as to the form of punishment but it may have been a caning or perhaps they were made to stand in a corner of the classroom with backs to the rest of the class, hands on head, for the duration of the lesson. The three R's were not ignored and pupils were frequently examined in arithmetic, reading and tables.

Henrietta Clarke resigned in 1867 and Mary J. Bonwick commenced duties as Head Mistress on the 3rd June. This lady did not remain long at the school and one can only assume that her employment was temporary, for when the school closed for the Christmas vacation she recorded that her engagement had been fulfilled. During her short reign this lady's Log Book seems to indicate special concern over needlework, scripture and punishments.

Following the departure of Mary J. Bonwick, Miss Sophia Keats took over as Head Mistress on the 7th January 1868 at the beginning of the new term. The very bad weather that winter kept attendance low and those present were *"reproved for loud talking"*.

The Rectors of St. James' Church, leading townspeople and of course the School Inspectors, were frequent visitors to the school, for although the discipline seemed strict, the wellbeing of these children was very much of their concern. Whilst Miss Keats was Head Mistress, the School Inspector, Mr Gutch, had this to report *"This school is in a very fair state of general efficiency, the order is well kept and the instruction given with great care and satisfactory results. More books are required for the Upper Standards"*.

In 1877 yet another Head Mistress, A. Bryning, was appointed and was to remain Head of the school for the next two years. In his school report of 1879 Mr Gutch stated *"The instruction and discipline have fallen off in this school and improvement will be expected next year"*. In July Sarah H. Blackman became a newly appointed Head Mistress.

Despite the remarks made by Mr Gutch, the standard of education seems to have been fairly reasonable, for girls coming into the school at five years of age from the Infants' Department could count up to 100 and read and spell small words.

Shortly after Miss Alice Price took over as Head Mistress of St. James' Girls in October 1882, the syllabus was extended. In addition to the three R's the girls were now taught geography, history, physical exercises and elementary science. Needlework continued to be an important subject in the syllabus and was taught by Lizzy Larkman. Although very overcrowded, St. James' was undoubtedly a good school. The neatness of the paperwork, the capital needlework and the general intelligence were all noted by the School Inspectors. At the turn of the century Miss Laura Goff was Mistress (see photo taken about 1904/5).

Gertrude C. Glasson became Head Mistress in October 1921. The Log

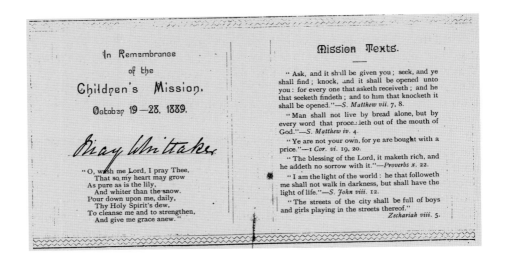

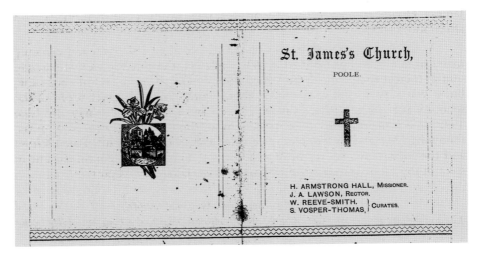

In Remembrance
of the
Children's Mission.
October 19—28, 1889.

Bray Whittaker

"O, wash me Lord, I pray Thee,
That so my heart may grow
As pure as is the lily,
And whiter than the snow.
Pour down upon me, daily,
Thy Holy Spirit's dew,
To cleanse me and to strengthen,
And give me grace anew."

Mission Texts.

"Ask, and it shall be given you; seek, and ye shall find; knock, and it shall be opened unto you: for every one that asketh receiveth; and he that seeketh findeth; and to him that knocketh it shall be opened."—*S. Matthew vii. 7, 8.*

"Man shall not live by bread alone, but by every word that proceedeth out of the mouth of God."—*S. Matthew iv. 4.*

"Ye are not your own, for ye are bought with a price."—*I Cor. vi. 19, 20.*

"The blessing of the Lord, it maketh rich, and he addeth no sorrow with it."—*Proverbs x. 22.*

"I am the light of the world: he that followeth me shall not walk in darkness, but shall have the light of life."—*S. John viii. 12.*

"The streets of the city shall be full of boys and girls playing in the streets thereof."
Zechariah viii. 5.

St. James's Church,

POOLE.

H. ARMSTRONG HALL, MISSIONER.
J. A. LAWSON, RECTOR.
W. REEVE-SMITH,
S. VOSPER-THOMAS, } CURATES.

St James' Childrens Mission October 1889. Card in the name of May, older sister of Vera Whittaker mother of the author.

for 1923 records that two weddings took place. One was a royal occasion, when the Duke of York was married on the 26th April, but of greater consequence to the school was the marriage of Miss Glasson in November, bringing her Head Mistresship to an end.

Miss Glasson was succeeded by Miss Gladys M. Harding, who remained Head of the school until 1939, when she transferred to the new Henry Harbin Secondary Modern Girls' School. For the greater part of the time that Miss Harding was Head Mistress the infants at St. James' were in the charge of Miss R. A. Cross, but in 1934 the girls' and the infants' were amalgamated and as from November of that year, Miss Harding was appointed Head Mistress in charge of the whole school.

All the celebrations that were always associated with a royal event in those days took place in 1935 on the occasion of the Silver Jubilee of King George V and Queen Mary. During June the annual Elementary School Sports took place, which was also the time of the very well attended Poole Carnival. During the year, St. James' girls won 8 honours certificates in a national needlework competition.

The declaration of war with Germany took place during the latter part of the summer holidays in 1939 and when school resumed in September, the position of Head Mistress was given to Louise Rendall. Because of the uncertainty over the war and the need to take precautions, schooling at first took place in the afternoons only from 1 p.m. to 4.30 p.m. After a while the old building was closed temporarily and the junior girls attended Henry Harbin School with Miss Rendall and some of the infants were transferred to Lagland Street. Children from the other side of Poole Bridge attended Hamworthy School, leaving only 79 children remaining on the roll at St. James'. However, in October school resumed normally with morning and afternoon sessions.

As the war progressed, Poole started to experience air raids and certainly many air raid warnings and during 1940 and 1941, the children were frequently sent to their shelters, usually only for a period of a quarter of an hour at a time, but it was very disruptive for their school work. Then an upper room of the school was burnt out during an air raid on the night of Wednesday, 3rd June 1942. It was necessary to close the school for the rest of the week and on the following Monday, the juniors were using two rooms in South Road school and the infants two rooms in Lagland Street. The air raids continued but in spite of this a nursery class had re-started in St. James' by August.

St James' Girls' (Poole Girls' National) 1904/5.
Class of infants with teacher Miss Crabbe, Head Mistress Miss Laura Goff just visible in the doorway. Names recalled, Ethel Thomas, Nellie Kerley, Reg Wilkins, Marie Harwood.

1939 – Party held in the Old Guildhall, Market Street in honour of Miss Harding who had been appointed Headmistress at the new Henry Harbin School. Seated with Miss Harding are her mother, Mayor Joe Bright and Mrs Bright, Mr. Albert Goff, Alderman Carter and Mrs Carter. Names recalled: Rev'd Arthur White, Miss Shear, Miss Lydford, Miss Ballet, Miss Bollom, Mrs Hancock, Margaret Reeves, Bowers, Geary, Young, Wellstead, Hurst and Withers.

In September 1943 Alderman Carter, Chairman of the Education Committee, presented the school with a Certificate of Honour for the Wings for Victory Week. He commended the pupils on the standard of their work, particularly in view of the fact that they had been more disturbed by the war than most schools in the area. The old Poole Girls' National School became **St. James' Junior Girls' and Infants' School** in April 1945 and Miss Rendall continued as Head Mistress until her resignation in July 1947, which was the year when the very old school was eventually closed down.

The population of the old town was gradually moving out to the developing districts of Oakdale, Parkstone and Broadstone. Poole Old Town was now left with the Lagland Street Infants' School, which accommodated children of both sexes up to the age of seven and South Road School which took over from there until the child attended either Grammar School or a Secondary Modern School, as determined by the 11+ examination.

Group 1, 1914 with Miss Ballet
Names recalled: Battrick, Hilda Edwards, Dolly Phillips, Cartridge, Weldon, Wellstead,
Ethel Thomas, Marie Harwood, Daisy Beament.

St. James Girls School – June 1914
School Tableau 'Entente Cordiale'. Entered in Poole Carnival and won First Prize.
Britannia was portrayed by E. Thomas. The 'English' were in mop caps. The 'French' were
in white bonnets. and all carried traditional flowers. At the judging, everyone shook hands in
friendship. Other names recalled: Beament, Edwards, Phillips.

BRITISH SCHOOL, FOR GIRLS,
LAGLAND STREET, POOLE.

OPEN TO ALL CLASSES.

THIS School has been re-opened, after the Christmas Holidays, and placed under Miss BOTTEREL, a new Mistress, educated in the School of the British and Foreign School Society, with the advantage of three years' subsequent experience in a large School in the North of England.

Complaints have been made by Parents, that too little time is devoted to *Needle-work*. The Managers of the School have, after due consideration, resolved on such alterations, as cannot fail to meet the wishes of the Parents, without injury to the interests of the Children.

The following will be the arrangement of the GIRLS' School, commencing from the 11th of January instant:—

HOURS OF ATTENDANCE:

IN THE MORNING,..........NINE TO TWELVE.
IN THE AFTERNOON,—
    MICHAELMAS to LADY-DAY,..TWO TO FOUR.
    LADY-DAY to MICHAELMAS,..TWO TO FIVE.

COURSE OF INSTRUCTION:

Reading, Writing, Arithmetic, Geography, &c.
THE AFTERNOON WILL BE DEVOTED TO *NEEDLE-WORK*.

TERMS:

For a **SINGLE CHILD**, - - - **TWO-PENCE per Week.**
For **TWO SISTERS**, - - - - **THREE-PENCE per Week.**
For **THREE SISTERS**, - - - **FOUR-PENCE per Week.**

Representations have been made to the Managers of complaints by some Parents, that the rule for punctual attendance at the prescribed hours, is too rigidly enforced: the Managers, whilst feeling that some allowance in this respect should occasionally be made *in the Girls' School*, most earnestly press the Parents' assistance, in forming in the children habits of order and punctuality.

The School will be regularly visited by Ladies, feeling an interest in the Institution.

M. K. WELCH, *Secretary.*

POOLE, *January 1st*, 1847.

Lankester, Printer, Poole.

Poole British School Rules and List of Subscribers — July 1846.

British School, Skinner Street

When the new Congregational Chapel was built in Skinner Street in 1777 at a cost of £1,400, the old chapel was adapted for use as a Sunday School and also for use as school rooms in the week. This building, fronting Lagland Street, cost £374. 7s. 7d. (the bill is still preserved) in 1760. It was demolished during the 1980's much to the dismay of local folk, many of whom thought it should be preserved. The main part of the site is now a car park for the church. However, the original tessellated tiling which served as the entrance to the original chapel – for which James Oliver was paid 7/6d in 1760 – has been left in situ in a small reserved area adjoining Lagland Street by the church noticeboards.

The Sunday School in it is connected with John Clench, famous for later introducing vaccination to North America. He knew both Robert Raikes (pioneer of the Sunday School Movement) and Edward Jenner (pioneer of vaccination) from earlier days in Gloucester. In Poole he brought sixteen children from Hamworthy by boat to St James' in 1787, but the churchwardens, already having many poor on their books, refused admission blaming the inconvenience they would cause pewholders (including the Lester family, who ironically had supported his earlier work as a doctor in Newfoundland). Clench took the children to Skinner Street, where they were welcomed and formed the nucleus of a flourishing Sunday School. (Ordained later that year, John Clench served St Paul's Anglican Church, Trinity until his death.)

Boys, girls and babies were taken under the wing of voluntary teachers, who were responsible for instructing the children. The education was scanty, but attempts were made to give the rudiments to neglected children. The generosity of certain members of the congregation of the church, British and Foreign Bible Society subscriptions, and the childrens' weekly one penny or two pennies were the only sources of income.

Because of the lack of funds, the quality of the teaching was not always of the best. A scanty education was to be preferred to no education at all, and this establishment began to prosper. An enlargement undertaken in 1833 accommodated the Lancastrian Free School for Boys. This was run on a monitorial system with one master (at one time Henry Whicher) and 120 boys. The master taught the senior boys, who in turn taught the junior boys, and so on. This school eventually languished through lack of funds because they were loath to accept State aid. After a temporary closure in 1844 the

POOLE BRITISH SCHOOLS.

RULES.

1.—The internal management of the Schools, that is to say, the general routine of Instruction and Discipline shall be conducted on the system already adopted, which is that usually in operation in the Schools of the British and Foreign School Society.

2.—The external control of the School, that is to say, the care of the Funds, the payment, choice, and dismissal of Masters and Mistresses, and the care and management of the Rooms and Premises used for the Schools, shall be vested in six Managers, viz., a President, Treasurer, two Vice-Presidents, and two lady Vice-Presidents for the special affairs of the Girls' School. The Treasurer shall act as Secretary.

3.—In addition to the Managers (who will be Visitors *ex-officio*), twenty-four Visitors shall be appointed, viz., twelve ladies as Visitors of the Girls' School, and twelve gentlemen as Visitors of the Boys' School, in order that a constant inspection of the working of the Schools may be maintained.

4.—An Annual Meeting of the Subscribers to the Schools shall be held previous to the Midsummer Examination, of which due notice shall be given, and at which an account of the receipts and expenditure for the foregoing year, and a report of the state of the Schools shall be read, and visitors shall be chosen for the ensuing year. And once in every three years, at such Annual Meeting, the President, Treasurer, and Vice-Presidents shall be chosen.

5.—The Managers shall be chosen from among the Subscribers in the following manner: Each Subscriber having been furnished with a printed or written list of the Subscribers, shall mark those who appear suitable for the respective Offices, and sign his or her name, and these papers being given to the Chairman of the Meeting, (who on this occasion must not be one of the Managers) he shall declare the result. And if any one chosen as a Vice-President shall decline to act, or if a vacancy should occur between the Annual Meetings, the other Manager shall fill up the vacancy, and their appointment shall be confirmed, or a new one made, at the next General Meeting. But the President and Treasurer shall be chosen only at a General Meeting of the Subscribers, and if necessary, a Meeting shall be specially called for that purpose.

6.—The Visitors shall be chosen from among the Subscribers in the following manner:— The Treasurer shall read and propose a list to the Meeting, in which it shall be open to any Subscriber to propose any alteration, and such proposal and the original list shall be adopted or rejected by the vote of the Meeting.

7.—These Rules shall not be rescinded, altered, or added to, except by the vote of two-thirds of such Subscribers as shall be present at a General Meeting, notice having been given to each Subscriber, at least one month previous to such Meeting, of the exact nature and extent of the proposed alteration.

At a Meeting of the Subscribers held at the School Room, the 26th of June, 1846;

IT WAS PROPOSED AND RESOLVED,

That the Rev. E. R. Conder be the President of the School.

Also, that Mr. M. K. Welch be Treasurer and Secretary.

That the following Gentlemen be Vice-Presidents for the Boys:—G. L. Parrott, and William Binns, Esqrs.

That the following Ladies be Vice-Presidents:—Miss Thompson and Miss Coward.

That the following Ladies and Gentlemen be Visitors of the Schools for the year ensuing:—

FOR THE BOYS.	FOR THE GIRLS.
Rev. Thomas Durant,	Mrs. Brown,
Mr. J. Brown,	Mrs. J. Durant,
Mr. Durant,	Mrs. Lancaster,
Mr. Lancaster,	Mrs. Salter,
Mr. Joseph Knight,	Mrs. Aldridge,
Mr. Vernon,	Mrs. Ayling,
Mr. Harding,	Mrs. Welstead,
Mr. H. M. Aldridge,	Mrs. Hixey,
Mr. Scott,	Mrs. Knight,
Mr. Samuel Humby,	Miss Green (Oxford),
Mr. Thomas Nash,	Miss Penney,
Mr. White (High Street).	Miss Selby.

At a Meeting of the Managers held the 20th of July, 1846,

THE FOLLOWING RESOLUTIONS WERE ADOPTED:

That the Managers meet on the first Monday in every month, at 11 o'Clock in the forenoon, to receive the report of the School for the past month, the first Meeting to take place on the first Monday in September.

That no other business shall be transacted at such Monthly Meetings, unless either the President or Treasurer, and two others besides himself, shall be present.

That the Rules of the School be printed, with a list of the Managers and Visitors.

Mr. Binns having declined to act as one of the Vice-Presidents, on account of advanced age,—

RESOLVED,

That Mr. John Brown be requested to supply his place for the year ensuing.

Lankester, Printer, High-Street, Poole.

school carried on with boys and girls attending separately under the one heading of British.

Religious prejudice, not least in Poole, had caused strong opposition to Sir James Graham's 1843 Factory Bill which proposed state-built, church-run schools and aimed at giving child workers some education, yet the need for schools was great. With the aim of meeting the need the motto of the British School became *"Open to all - belonging exclusively to none"*.

In 1847, Miss Botterel became the Headmistress of the Girls' School, and at the parents' request needlework was given much prominence on the curriculum (See illustrations).

The reasons given for boys leaving school in November 1849 varied from "work" to "no boots to wear". Charles Angel was obviously ill-named for he was "dismissed".

The school survived only while Martin Kemp-Welch (described on his death in 1884 as "the school's best friend"), subsidised it. In 1867 under Government inspection, it qualified for an annual grant and reopened. The boys' section flourished to such an extent that a further extension was built and came into use in 1880. The 300 boys were under the Headmastership of Thomas Perry Hicks from Liskeard, Cornwall. He found that the boys came to school sporting oak leaves on Royal Oak day (29th May) and explained its significance.

The 198 girls and infants for less than a year were under Miss A. Whadcoat, who was followed by Miss E. Lowe who remained in the position of Headmistress until 1912, when she transferred to the new South Road school for a short period. Miss Lowe had a stern exterior but underneath, for those in her favour, she showed a deal of kindness. She was short of stature and wore the role of mistress befittingly in a long black gown which covered her shoes. Circular steel rimmed spectacles sat primly on her nose and her hair always was brushed upwards all around and pinned up in a tight knot or bun on top. She did not suffer fools lightly and any girls whom she considered slow or stupid were unceremoniously pummelled in their backs around the classroom. If they happened to be wearing spectacles, which dropped off in the process, she seemed never to notice but just kept on pummelling away until her venom was out. The other girls in the class were far too scared to laugh, or cry for that matter, for punishment was always quick to follow any behaviour which was not completely docile and sensible.

Prayers were always the first lesson of the day and were taken in the Hall. Any latecomers were made to stand outside of the door until prayers had finished and then, to the accompaniment their fellow scholars singing "The Voice of the Sluggard", they were made to proceed in disgrace to the front of the assembly. As many of the poor children were made to run errands and do jobs before attending school, this morning humiliation was a frequent occurrence. As at the St. James' Girls' School, needlework lessons were quite on an even footing with the three R's and in order that grubby or damp hands should not soil the work, the girls were made to rub their hands frequently in

December, 18 4 9

Number on the books at end of last month	166
Admitted since	10
Number left	12
Now on the books	164
Average attendance	115

Remarks.

Names of those who have left.	Cause of leaving.
Rowland Foote, William Flipping	Errols
Thomas Matthews, James Matthews	Parents Can't afford to pay
Thomas Fordh, William Sulthist	-3 years given
George Garland, Joseph Pervent	Errols
Edwd Colins, Thos Mulay	Taken away because sent home after money
William Exay	Parents Can't afford to pay schooling
Thomas Fletcher	No reason given

December 1849 – Reasons for leaving school. One was that the parents could not afford the two-pence per week fee for schooling.

"flour" during the needlework classes.

Thomas Perry Hicks, the Boys' Head, died on the 4th November,1881, aged 42 years and was followed by James Reynish who found some of the classes very backward. He improved matters by introducing Drawing (attracting a grant from South Kensington), drill and home lessons. Singing was also commended at inspectors' inspections. He sought parental help to combat truancy, threatening expulsion, for keeping up average attendances was a factor in assessing grant. Even so the school had to be closed by order of the MOH in 1892 when measles raged in the town. In 1886 he had to deal with fears of smallpox, then prevalent, keeping boys from school.

He resolved to avoid "sticking" boys as far as possible, offering marks for punctuality and attendance which led to rewards. Even so he could not prevent boys absenting themselves when the town was in a state of excitement at the dreadful murder of Alderman Hamilton in 1886. When a street brawl broke out with boys of the National School up the road he gave the miscreants' names to the police, hoping that a *"friendly feeling may exist between the two schools"*. Reynish was thirty years Headmaster of the school, from 1882 until 1912, the year in which the leaving age for pupils was raised from 13 to 14 years and also the year South Road School opened. He continued as Head of the new South Road School and died on the 2nd November 1914 aged 67 years. Many years later, his desk was still there at the British with the cane at its side, just as many a boy had reason to recall it, ready for punishment, which was levied swiftly and often.

The British School Log Book from 1867 was handed, at his request, to the Town Clerk in 1931. In the 1900's a new code came into operation with a new syllabus which consisted of Reading, Recitation, Writing, Composition, Grammar, Arithmetic, Geography, History, Science (easy mechanics and chemistry) with experiments, Drawing, Singing, P.E. with dumb-bells and Alexander's Drill. The same subjects were taken by all the boys and girls in the Classes I to Vl with the subject matter getting progressively harder with each upward class.

In the year 1900 there were 253 boys attending the British School. Of these, 42 were infants. This was well within the limits allowed in light of the measurements of the school rooms which were as follows:

No 1 Room 37' x 35' = 1295 sq. ft. = Accommodation for 162

No 2 Room 37' x 24' = 888 sq. ft. = Accommodation for 111

No 3 Room 12' x 19' = 228 sq. ft. = Accommodation for 28

Total accommodation available for 301 pupils

The staff at that time, under the Headmaster James Reynish, were Frank Wheeler (lst class certificate) Thomas Briscoe, Mary Chaffey and Josephine Potter and Edgar Ralph (P.T.)

The report for the year read *"Discipline of Boys School very quiet and well maintained. Good progress in elementary work, singing improved. Class subjects taught by good methods and results are intelligent. Drawing well taught and model drawing above average"*.

In early 1901, Mr Reynish was concerned at poor attendances on account of the severe cold weather and snowstorms, which necessitated closure of school for a couple of days.

In March of that year an outbreak of ringworm among pupils sufficed to make its entry in the Log Book. In early May, Poole Fair held in Market Place caused a drop in attendance and on the 11th June a combination of the Headmaster's faceache and a circus visiting town caused school to be closed half a day in the afternoon. Three days later a demonstration held on the return of the Dorset Volunteers from South Africa and the combination of Sunday school treats was the cause of yet another afternoon's holiday. In July Mr H. B. Elford became a new school correspondent to assist J. P. Godwin.

By September, chemistry lessons were well under way. They were being taken by Mr Wheeler and an aid grant was received for the purchase of scientific apparatus and chemicals. However, by the 20th September Mr Wheeler told the Headmaster that he had been offered £10 per annum more than he was getting at the British school and Headmaster asked if he could hold back and await the next visit of H.M. Inspectors, when he would try to get his salary raised accordingly. The Inspectors were expected at any time, but Mr Wheeler went ahead with his resignation as from 1st November. Just one week after Mr Wheeler had talked to the Headmaster, Miss Chaffey approached him and asked for a rise in salary. Mr Reynish took the matter up with the correspondent, but before the matter was resolved Miss Chaffey had to leave on account of ill health. When Mr Wheeler left on 1st November he was presented with a beautiful copy of Browning's Poems and the following day Sidney Sampson started to replace him.

In November Mr E. S. Mostyn-Pryce, H.M. Inspector of Schools, called and in his report he stated *"Boys' school is well organised"* but he ends up by saying *"the employment of two female assistants in the male department does not seem wholly desirable"*. The Drawing Inspector, Mr Arthur W. Geffeken, suggested that the use of paper or books instead of slates was to be strongly recommended.

Despite HM Inspector's remarks, it was necessary to employ yet another

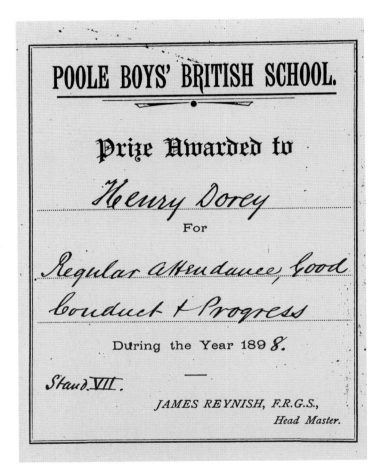

Henry Dorey's prize was a leather-bound, gold-embossed, well illustrated book entitled 'Half Hours at Sea' — stories of Voyage, Adventure and Wreck — It included in its pages a lurid true tale of Piracy in Poole Harbour!

A school outing group in the early 1900's which includes Miss Jeffrey, Miss Lowe and Miss Arnold. Names recalled: Brown, Wilkins, Whitty.

female member of staff, as the advertised post attracted no male applicants. Miss Bessie Williams commenced duties in April 1902.

At this time, Sergeant Houghton R.A. acted as Drill Instructor to classes of 30 boys from the top standards, and those attending very much enjoyed the drill as recommended by H.M. Inspector. Obviously with only three rooms to work in and six classes of children to teach, there was a necessity to share the rooms and in addition the Infants' School was held in the first floor rooms and the noise from above was often distracting to the children trying to take their lessons on the ground floor. Very often during the winter when many of the children had severe colds and coughs, the noise of the coughing became intolerable and the Headmaster often complained of headaches because of it.

The Boer War had ended by June 1902 and then the King was taken seriously ill. All local festivities were postponed and then an epidemic of measles necessitated closure of school for 6 weeks on instructions from the Medical authorities. The boys took this opportunity to go out fishing in the harbour, as many of the families were fisher-folk.

In October of 1902, Mayor Charles Carter presented the school with 12 copies of Mr Gill's *"Sketches of the Past of Poole"* in the hope that it would engender the love of history.

The staff now consisted of Thomas Briscoe, Sidney Sampson, Josephine Potter, Bessie Williams and Edgar Ralph, with James Reynish still their Headmaster, who was of the opinion that all of them were *"earnest and diligent*

British School Poole No II – 1897
Class with teacher and pupil-teacher. Names recalled: Blanche Allen,
Iris Munden, Elsie Allen.

in their application". However, on November 24th the Inspector visited and complained of the lack of light and once again of the employment of female assistants.

Total aid grants in November was £140 which was to pay the salaries of the teachers in the Boys' Section amounting to £66.10.0d. and the Girls' Section £39.0.0d. and in the Infants' £34.10.0d.

On the 5th January, 1903 Mr Arthur L. Young commenced duties as an assistant and on the 27th a Mr Percy Smith commenced, but he stayed for only just a week and was paid the sum of £2.0.0d. Then a Mr Clifford Richards was appointed as from the 28th February. The staffing situation was to be a problem for the Headmaster because the Inspectors insisted that the female assistants were to be told that they should leave as soon as it was convenient. On the 20th March a Mr Arthur Palmer commenced duties and his reign was not to be for long either for he left in June.

In the light of the 1902 Education Act the future of the school was discussed by the Managers, who called a meeting of subscribers. It was unanimously recommended that the school be made a Provided School by transfer; in the meantime things must carry on as usual and in April another Guardian was elected. Staff problems worsened to the extent that the Headmaster's son, James Bruce, was engaged for two weeks at the end of July. He was there when Miss Potter left with a presentation of a silver toast rack and a water colour painting on porcelain. On the last day of term, the noise overhead from the children's tea party in the room above was so unbearable the Headmaster decided to break up early.

When school re-opened in August after the summer break, a Mr Rob Overton started as an assistant. It seems that he was far from satisfactory from the Headmaster's point of view, who complained that he had to be watched and cautioned and that he stood too much by the fire and was generally lazy and in the habit of beating the boys, sometimes without sufficient cause. Mr Reynish was not sorry when Mr Overton eventually gave a month's notice on 1st July 1904.

Truancy was always a great problem and it was felt that the judiciary was not giving sufficient support to the teachers and attendance officers.

Some of the children were very distressed on arrival at school on the morning of January 29th 1904, having witnessed an outbreak of fire at the Medical Aid House in Mount Street just as they were on their way to school. However, it was all forgotten by the time the arrival of three dual desks and a pedestal table with ink trays interested and excited the children a few days later.

Such was the closeness in the compact small community in those days that any joy or sadness that befell one seemed to affect them all. The grief was shared when one of the boys, Willie George Foot, from Standard IV died whilst undergoing an operation on July 1st. Then again in September the whole school mourned the death of Mr J.P. Godwin, who had been correspondent of the school for 24 years.

Staffing and attendance problems still persisted and the Headmaster gave the school a good talking to regarding attendance before a prize distribution for proficiency and certificates for those who did attend regularly. It seemed that one of the reasons for poor attendance was that every time the National School just up the road was granted a half day's holiday for good attendance, some of the boys at the British felt they should follow suit, especially if they had friends there.

To encourage the boys to attend more regularly, reward cards for a week's perfect attendance were distributed from September 1905. Just after their inception, on September 14th, school closed down for a day so that all could join the town in paying their last respects to the late Rector of Poole, Reverend Archibald Lawson.

The amalgamation of Poole and Branksome was celebrated in November 1905 when school was closed by order of the Education Committee. At the commencement of 1906, the Member of Parliament, Mr Lyall, visited town and as any visit by a notable caused a great deal of interest, the attendance at school dropped correspondingly. Mr Reynish continued in his encouragement of good attendance and on February 23rd he distributed 80 caps with the P.B.S. Badge to boys who attended 95% last year and 10 to boys of Standard I who had never missed since they started at the British School.

Late 1800's. Group 1 of the British Girls School with Miss Lowe, Headmistress, and possible a young Miss Jeffery when she was an assistant teacher.

The Inspector of Cruelty to Children visited school on April 6th and Mr Reynish was glad to have his co-operation. This was in connection with the case against Caroline Knight, who had been accused of neglecting her children. Headmaster was to be a witness in June when she pleaded Guilty and was sentenced to two months' hard labour and the children were sent to the Union (in Longfleet Road, now the St Mary's Unit).

At the end of April four boys from Standard VII sat the Labour Exams at St Peter's, Parkstone at mid-day; three of them passed and left school. In May the local residents used the school rooms as a Polling Station for Polls to decide (for or against) purchase of the Waterworks. On the 6th July Bostock and Wombwell's Menagerie visited town. School was dismissed at 3.15 p.m. to allow the teachers to take the classes at two pence per head.

On the re-opening of school after the summer break, measles were prevalent and attendance once again was low. Fetes at Brownsea Island did not help matters for many of the children stayed away from school to attend. In early November the Headmaster was summoned for Jury Service at Dorchester Assizes so the school was closed all the week.

In January of 1907, half a ton of coal was delivered to school, snow was falling and many outside activities were curtailed. However, medals for attendance were distributed at the beginning of January; two dozen First Class for perfect attendance, three dozen Second Class for attendance 400-410 times and three dozen Third Class for attendances of 95% and 15 books for proficiency and good conduct were given out. In spite of these incentives to perfect the attendance, the situation got worse and worse and the Headmaster seemed to think that the Magistrates were not backing up the Attendance Officers where 'sick notes' were concerned and expulsion was no longer the threat it had been when schooling was voluntary.

In May there was a United Concert by the Elementary Schools of the Borough in Amity Hall in High Street on behalf of the local hospital and the teachers' Benevolent & Orphans' Fund. This was so successful that it was repeated the following year.

Headmaster was pleased to note in September that two boys, Harold Clarke, Standard Vll and Edward Collington, Sixth Form, secured scholarships for the Secondary School but he continued to be discontented on account of the very bad attendance of the boys. In September he suggested that the Woodbury Hill Fair and fine weather for blackberrying caused some boys to abscond. In addition he was also very displeased with his teaching staff and there seems to have been quite a turnover of those. For example, in November Mr Viggers and Mr Sargent were told off for taking the timetables and daily record books home so that they were not available at school. In 1908 he commenced a Register of Punctuality of Attendance for the staff and they had to sign on and off at each attendance.

The weather was bitterly cold and many of the children were desperately ill, two boys, W. Norris (Class 4) and Percy Knight (Class 3) died. The noise from the incessant coughing troubled the masters greatly, concentration was difficult. It seems to have been a very unhappy time for the school, for the Inspectors when they visited criticised Mr Reynish for not bringing the benefit of his experience to the young and inexperienced staff. However, he still tried to encourage good attendance and the prizes given out in March consisted of 84 caps with the red initials P.B.S. and 22 books for efficiency. All were presented by Herbert Saunders, the Sheriff, and a half day's holiday was awarded.

The building really was very inadequate for schooling purposes and the Managers met in April to discuss the Inspectors' report on the building but they resolved to reply to the Education Committee that, being tenants, they could not carry out the suggestions of the Board of Education report which had been received earlier.

By 1908 Mr Reynish was certainly a very sick man and almost everything seems to have irritated him. He complained so much of all of his staff and, for example, of Harry Tandy (Class 3) he complains *"he lacks energy and speaks too low"*. Another incident which annoyed him greatly was when Mr Herbert S. W. Burroughs sent a note to regret that he was not able to resume duties for a few days as he was run down consequent upon a severe strain. This note had been sent from an address in Bath and Mr Reynish replied to the same address. He was very surprised when his letter was returned by a Mr Burroughs who stated that he knew no Herbert S.W. Burroughs in Bath or district.

Headmaster summoned the Managers to consider the matter, for Mr Burroughs had asked for and received an advance on his vacation salary. It was agreed that he had broken his engagement with the school and to pay him up to 31st August and terminate his engagement. It was afterwards learned that the "strain" from which Mr Burroughs was suffering was that he had appeared before the Bath Magistrates on a charge of obtaining board and lodgings (value 27/-) by false pretences. He was found innocent.

In October 1908 the school joined the Poole School's Football League, so Mr Townsend took the boys out for practice at 4 p.m. on Thursday afternoons, weather permitting.

The report for 1908 from H.M. Inspectors stated that *"the school was making steady progress towards efficiency"*. The question of school accommodation was beginning to press seriously, although the numbers on the books were cut down from 312 to 160 in 1909. Despite the Headmaster's complaints about attendance, in March the Mayor, Ald. Ballard, distributed prizes for good attendance and five of the boys had never been absent for several years. The Mayor presented a half sovereign which was to be distributed amongst them. In addition he presented 95 paintboxes, 2 dozen crayons and 5 caps.

In June the attendance had dropped to 111, as scarlet fever was rife and one of the scholars, Bertie Barnes was sent to the Fever Hospital at Baiter. In the middle of June a hundred boys attended the Bostock and Wombwell's Menagerie to receive object lessons on listed animals and on the 28th Mr Townsend for the first time took the VI and VII Standards to the Park for the first trial lesson of the outdoor syllabus. The boys measured the cricket ground and studied two or three trees, this all under the heading of Arithmetic and Nature Study. The first experimental lesson seems to have been successful for it was continued throughout the summer of 1909.

After the summer break, the attendance was bad again and apparently some of the boys left for hop fields and would be away for quite some weeks. Poole Regatta and Woodbury Hill Fair were blamed for poor attendance.

Again in early 1910 the attendance suffered, this time on account of electioneering. There were political meetings on the Quay and at the end of January the Liberal procession on the Quay with Lady Wimborne, Winston Churchill, MP, and Dr. MacNamara attracted many Poole residents. Conservative followers flocked to the Station to meet Lord Beresford and his entourage. On 27th January the school was used as a Polling Station for the election and the following day the Headmaster took the ballot box up to Wimborne in the morning and was very disappointed to find only 153 boys present on his return. The excitement and disruption of the classes at the event of an election would not be understood today.

In May another very interesting event took place on the Quay when a Wild Bear Show visited and many of the boys absented themselves from school on this account. In the same month King Edward Vll died and George V was proclaimed King. Bournemouth Centenary Celebrations

1906 – How proud Reginald Lugg would have been to receive this Regular Attendance Certificate from his Head, Mr. Reynish. Less than 10 years later he was dead. Killed in action at Jutland in 1916 at the age of 18.

caused the school to close for a week at the end of July and after the summer holiday when school resumed in September some of the children had to stay back at the Infants' Department at Rattray's because of the lack of accommodation at the British. Apart from the lack of teaching space, the cloakrooms were a continuing source of annoyance, especially on wet days with nowhere to dry the children's coats. They were so dark that sometimes a little classroom had to be used instead to enable the children to see to find their clothes. It was necessary to beg clothes and boots for some of the poorer children from the wealthier members of school.

On the 22nd and 23rd June 1911 school closed for the Coronation celebrations. There followed an epidemic of measles and the Infants' Section was closed in order that the Ministry of Health could disinfect the premises.

In September a resolution was passed to take steps to secure an extension of service by the Headmaster. In November the school was busy taking stock up to the new South Road School, furniture was carted there ready to be painted to look like new and on 20th December all the books were taken up to the new school. Boys broke up for Christmas looking forward to resumption of schooling in the New Year at their brand new schoolrooms.

1904/5 Infants class 2 with Miss Rattray.

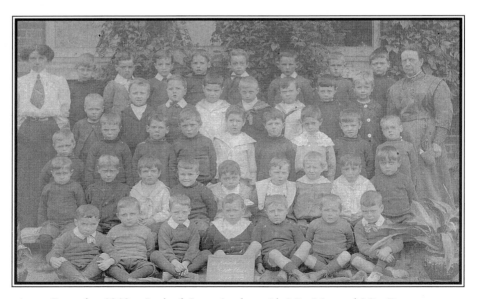

September 1912 – Lagland Street 1st class with Miss May and Miss Rattray.

Lagland Street Infants' School (Rattray's)

The British Chapel Lane Infants' School was built in 1793 and enlarged in 1843. There are no details recorded of the school until 1884, when it was opened in the old Wesleyan Chapel as a day school on the 7th January with 44 pupils, 20 boys and 24 girls present.

Miss Isabel Rattray was Headmistress and she had this to say about the accommodation: *"A very large building with no playground, no classrooms, no cupboards, a stove that would only heat properly if the wind was in one quarter. It is airy in summer but a terrible place to teach in".*

No records had been kept before 1884; as Miss Rattray wrote: *"The official portfolio of this school is empty. It should contain official correspondence and papers which relate to the Infants' School and should be ready for inspection. There are four new desks but more will be needed and there is no apparatus in view of the course of manual exercises and occupations indicated under Article 106/b/3."*

The number on the register was forty-nine and most of the children had transferred from the Skinner Street Congregational British School. Miss Rattray seemed to approve of their standard of reading and spelling but she considered their writing and arithmetic rather below standard. Her Log Book continues: *"Twenty per cent of those examined were over 7 years of age and presented as infants. Children over 7 years of age should as a rule be prepared for the first standard but the Mistress has only one monitor present. There is no satisfactory playground and the space available is of little service unless the three inside rows of railings are removed. Except as a temporary measure, the buildings are not thoroughly satisfactory in view of the present requirements of an Infants' School.*

In view of this report to HM Inspector on the premises of the Infants' School, I always hope to learn that the Managers will soon be able to provide more suitable buildings".

School continued in these unsatisfactory buildings, Miss Rattray introducing a new timetable, there being no Standard I in the school. The Reverend Ebenezer Evans, from the Congregational Church at Skinner Street, was a fairly frequent visitor. Many of the children of his flock came to this school and after Easter of 1884, seven more children from the Skinner Street British School started at Miss Rattray's at Chapel Lane. She was pleased to note in April that Isabel Loader began her duties as monitress, but expressed doubts of her abilities as *"She had been educated at a small private school".*

Miss Rattray seemed not to have been one to have minced her words, for at the end of May of that year when a circus came to town and she allowed

Back row: Miss Hart, B. Hescoff, J. Cosh, Gillingham, N. Young, W. Houlton,
D. Tilsed, Miss M. Brooks. 2nd row: Batt, R. Baker, S. Vick, H. Neville, J. Vine,
M. Othen, J. Amey, E. Miles. 3rd row: L. Walwood, V. Almer, G. Woodward,
C. Giles, Ford, Cutler, N. Kearley. Front row: H. Marsh, C. Bartlett, E. Power,
N. Coates, S. Willis.

the children a half day's holiday, she wrote in her Log Book, *"It is impossible to get a fair attendance when this is the case"*.

Several small improvements were carried out on the buildings over the next few years; a new gallery was installed which proved quite a considerable help in teaching the growing number of pupils, but eventually Miss Rattray's pleas were heard and a new Infants' School was built at Lagland Street in 1894. It was situated between the Boys' National at the top end of Perry Gardens and the British School lower down at the corner of Skinner Street.

Lagland Street School opened on the 2nd April 1894 for boys and girls numbering 222. On the previous Friday, tea had been supplied on the premises to the children who would be attending. One of the pupil teachers who moved up to help Miss Rattray was Miss Emile Wheeler. Unfortunately, soon after the opening an epidemic of Scarlet Fever broke out, but Miss Isabel Rattray was overjoyed with her new school.

Later (1901) she had this to say of it: *"How rejoiced we all were to come to our present rooms, how comfortable to have premises of our own, not sharing with others, to have a caretaker who tries to keep things clean and tidy, good fires on always when we get down to school on a winter morning and able to have plants and pictures to make the school look bright. I have been very happy in these rooms"*.

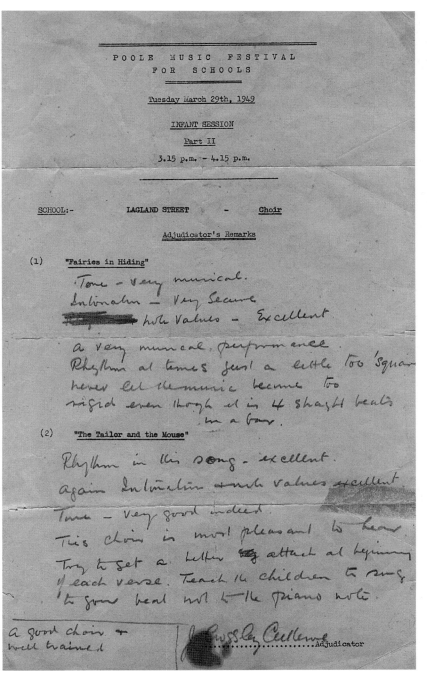

Tuesday March 29th, 1949

INFANT SESSION

Part II

3.15 p.m. – 4.15 p.m.

SCHOOL:- **LAGLAND STREET** – Choir

Adjudicator's Remarks

(1) "Fairies in Hiding"

Tone – very musical.
Intonation – Very Secure
~~note~~ Note Values – Excellent.

a very musical performance.
Rhythm at times just a little too 'square'
never let the music become too
rigid even though it is 4 straight beats
in a bar.

(2) "The Tailor and the Mouse"

Rhythm in this song – excellent.
Again Intonation + note values excellent.
Tone – Very good indeed.
This choir is most pleasant to hear.
Try to get a better attack at beginning
of each verse. Teach the children to sing
to your beat not to the piano note.

a good choir +
well trained

.... Crossley Cullew...............Adjudicator

1949 – The children, all under seven years of age were well commended as a good choir and well trained.

Borough of Poole Education Committee.

Lagland St .... School. .... *Infants* ... Dept.

REPORT.

Name *Blundell Doreen* .... Class *St I* .... Position ....

SUBJECTS.		MARKS.		GENERAL REMARKS.
		OBTD.	POSS.	
ENGLISH				
Composition	...	5	5	*Very satisfactory in*
Reading	...	5	5	*work & behaviour.*
Spelling	...			*Very nice character.*
Penmanship	...			
MATHEMATICS.				
Arithmetic	...	7	7	
GEOGRAPHY.		9		
HISTORY.	... ...	9		
ART.	... ...			
				C. Hughes
				Class Teacher.
scripture - Good				*G. E. Hart. L.LA.*
				Head Teacher.
	Total	...		

Reports in the 1930's more simple and to the point. This was that of the author, aged about 4½ years old. A far cry from the complications of today.

The average number of pupils attending in 1900 was 234 consisting of 229 children over 3 years of age, and 5 under 3 years old. The Infants' school by this time was working in these suitable new premises which was a great improvement in every way, and in November Miss Rattray wrote: *"We invited the boys' parents on Wednesday the 7th, and the girls' parents on Wednesday the 14th of November. Had a display of matting, knitting, as well as an entertainment"*.

It sounds like a very successful parent/teacher meeting. When school reopened in January 1901, the weather was so cold and snowy that very few babies attended, and on 8th January snow fell so heavily that school was closed for two days. On the proclamation of Edward VII as King on 24th January, a further half day's holiday was given. In 1903 a new classroom for the babies was opened, and the curriculum was extended to include needlework, drawing, singing, recitation, spelling, mental arithmetic, reading, writing and arithmetic. Miss Eva Neal from Dorchester was engaged as assistant in May of 1905. She was to become a backbone of the school. During 1906 a sad note crept in on 21st September, when a boy named Charlie Stone was run over and killed by a wagon outside the school at 4.20 p.m. The children collected the sum of fourteen shillings for a wreath.

Attendance at school was given great emphasis and prizes were given to those whose attendance excelled. The Registers were very scrupulously maintained and examined at frequent intervals by such names as Mr. Saul Buckley, Herbert Saunders, H. Dorsett and Rosa M. Coles. The number of children attending this school from 3 to 7 years old seems to have been held at around the 200 mark. The age breakdown in 1908 was as follows:

> 3 and under 4 years – 20 boys 19 girls
>
> 4 and under 5 years – 22 boys 23 girls.
>
> 5 and under 6 years – 40 boys 25 girls.
>
> 6 and under 7 years – 29 boys 20 girls.
>
> 7 and under 8 years – no boys, one girl.

In 1909 the intakes of the 3 year olds jumped to 35 boys and 34 girls, but as the Board of Education was keen to keep the average number under 210 the Committee advised the school to reduce the number of admissions of children under 4 years with that end in view. When it was necessary to reduce expenditure by £4.16.0. Miss Rattray decided to make the savings by doing without the new plasticine materials. The Great War was now in progress and the infants subscribed to a fund in aid of wounded soldiers; the sums of 11/– and 15/– were sent in 1915.

In July of that same year Miss Isabel Rattray retired and her place was taken by her sister, Maud Rattray LLA (Ladies Literate in the Arts), on the 30th August. It is quite apparent from the Log Book that Isabel still kept a great interest in the Lagland Street School, and was a frequent visitor. She also examined the Registers for her sister, and seems always to have found them correct. The winter of 1915 brought a change in assembly times from 2 p.m. to 1.30 p.m., and dismissals from 4 p.m. to the earlier time of 3.30 p.m. to enable the cleaners to sweep up in daylight. As there were no blinds to the school windows, artificial light was forbidden on regulations issued from the Naval Base on account of the war.

At the end of World War I in 1918, it is interesting to note that the Headmistress's salary was £14.11.8d. Diphtheria was still a notifiable disease, and any pupil who had been in contact with it was excluded from attendance at school. One such boy, excluded because his sister was suffering from the disease in 1920, was Willie Clark.

On 28th April 1922 Maud Rattray retired, and on 1st May Miss A. E.

1940 War-time billeting letter. Note: It is addressed to the Headmistress's home address and not to the school.

Hart commenced duties as Head. Miss Rattray, as had her sister before her, kept in close touch with the school becoming a frequent visitor as Inspector of Registers.

Whenever the 24th May came round, Empire Day was well and truly celebrated in all schools. Lagland Street was no exception, rendering a robust National Anthem and saluting the Union Jack. Each child was given a small flag to wave as the entire school marched around the playground. The afternoons were always granted as a half day holiday.

Quite a fair number of the children took advantage of saving into the

Boot Club. Miss Rattray in 1924 continued to call at school to collect their pennies and enter the amount on a card, which when sufficiently full of saved shillings was exchangeable at certain shoe shops in the town for a pair of boots or shoes.

The teachers from both St. James' Girls' School and the South Road Standard I took an interest in the girls likely to pass from Lagland Street to their schools in the new school year, which started then on 1st April.

In 1932 the premises were remodelled and extended, and the formal opening took place on 28th July. As late as 1936 schooling was still a very personalised affair between the authorities and the Head. For example, the Town Clerk, Mr Wilson Kenyon, addressed a letter regarding the formation of a nursery class to Miss Hart at her home, Oak Cottage, Broadstone, and not to the school.

Miss Hart together with Miss Goff had recently visited nursery classes in London and had brought the idea back. The necessary structural alterations were carried out, necessary equipment purchased after the Board of Education had given their approval, and the new nursery class started on 5th April 1937. By 1941 there were two nursery classes in charge of Misses Carey and Goff. During the war years the children played host to Infants from St. James' at times when their own school was bombed, and also to some of St. Mary's Roman Catholic School children.

On 1st October 1945 Miss M. M. Slattery became Headmistress, and on 26th November 1945 the school became the new **Lagland Street County Primary (Infants') School**, with children moving up to South Road School at the age of seven years.

When Miss W. C. Currey became Headmistress on 28th April 1952, the numbers on the roll stood at around 300. The school stood alone in the midst of the slum clearance and all the resultant building now taking place in the Old Town, mainly in the form of blocks of flats. The children from the demolished homes were being moved for the most part out to the new Waterloo Estate, and until the time their own Estate school was built the children were transported into Poole in three busloads each morning, and returned after school each day.

They were accommodated in eight classrooms. There was a small Hall in addition to Staff rooms and adequate cloakrooms. Each morning started with Assembly in the Hall, and prayers taken either by the Head or one of the staff. The Hall was also used for Physical Activities and for lunch time where approximately half the pupils ate the school dinners supplied in containers from a central kitchen.

During October 1954 it was deemed necessary to call the Ambulance to transport children home to Waterloo Estate after they had suffered severe attacks of diarrhoea. By November practically the entire school was down with the "bug" and the method of supplying the warmed-up dinners came under suspicion.

Miss M. A. Cutler took over the Headship on 2nd May 1955, and school days continued in much the same vein. Numbers on the roll of Lagland Street began to fall and by 1958 the Managers, Councillor Clapp, Alderman Brown, Mrs. Ballam, and Messrs Taylor, Chaffey, Rigler, Rose and Hartnell were proposing that a class be formed at Lagland Street for backward children made up of scholars aged over seven years from the South Road School. Three of the Lagland Street classrooms were used by the South Road Juniors' whose premises were bursting at the seams, on the understanding that they should not use the Lagland Street playground but walk the few hundred yards back to South Road for play periods and outdoor activities.

The School Sports were held at the Garland Road Sports Ground, and Mr. Condon transported children and equipment there in his Minuet Coaches. Parents and Managers swelled the crowd, and after the events were over Alderman Brown, Vice-Chairman of the Managers, presented Miss Cutler with a Poole Pottery Lamp and an electric steam iron - gifts from the children, staff, canteen staff, caretaker and cleaner. Later, tea was taken back at Lagland Street School by Miss Cutler, the staff and Managers. Miss Cutler was to take a post as Head of Heatherlands County Primary Infants' School, and before she left Lagland Street on 24th July 1958 the children and staff presented her with a beautiful bouquet of flowers and a cheque.

As the days of Lagland Street as an Infants' School were now numbered, it was decided that Miss D. M. White (the Deputy Head) should take over as temporary Head until the school closed down. Miss White had spent the whole of her teaching career at Lagland Street, and when she took up her appointment on 9th September 1958 the number of pupils had dropped to 100 exactly. However, she agreed to accommodate a class of remedial children from St. Mary's RC School on one afternoon a week. In November the school hours were brought into line with the Juniors, so that afternoon sessions were from 1.30 p.m. to 3.30 p.m.

There were now only four classes instead of eight, three classrooms were used by the South Road Juniors and the spare room was available for the Infants as a music and art room. The Hall was used for assembly, physical activities and meals. Two dining room assistants relieved the teaching staff with some of the supervisory duties during the dinner hour. The meals were delivered from a Central Kitchen, and were served at properly laid tables with beakers, cutlery, cruets and flowers. The older children waited on the others and sat at the ends of the tables.

Because part of the cloakrooms was reserved for the Juniors, the Infants found space a bit cramped but nevertheless the recent redecoration had made the surroundings bright and cheerful.

The old Poole, which surrounded the school, was rapidly being demolished to make way for flats. Most of the families with children who had been moved out of the old houses were accommodated on the Waterloo Estate. And so the school, first built in 1894 to carry on the traditions built up by Miss Rattray at the Wesleyan Infants' School in Chapel Lane, finally finished as a school in its own right in 1962.

From 6th September 1962 all the children went to South Road, and Lagland Street became an annexe of South Road School to help them through the accommodating of children brought in from the Turlin Moor and later the Canford Heath Estates.

Once those Estates were serviced by their own schools, Lagland Street no longer had any useful purpose to fulfil, and it succumbed to the rebuilding of Old Poole. On its site now stands yet another block of flats!

1947 – With the war safely over, chidren were encouraged to prevent road accidents with a Poster Competition, open to all schools in Poole.

Top: St. Mary's Roman Catholic Schoolroom 1955.
Joy Randall, Teacher with class of mixed children (she later became Deputy Head). The girls were knitting or sewing. The boys worked with raffia. Names recalled: Annette Singleton, David Moody, Anne Cull, George Gill.

1954 – St. Mary's School Playground, West Quay Road. A pupil 'Mark' dressed for his First Communion. The dilapidated state of the buildings is in stark contrast to his smart white turn out.

St Mary's Roman Catholic School

The early records of Poole's Roman Catholics show that they met in private houses for their worship until St Mary's Church was built in West Quay Road. It is not surprising to find that in the early days groups of children were taught by the priest in charge in his home, a farmhouse in Wimborne Road, with another group meeting in Upton House, the home of the Doughty family after 1829. As numbers increased, and with funds from the Doughty family and the Weld family of Lulworth, a Roman Catholic school was erected in 1850 in New (or Norton) Road, next to the old Police Station in Market Street, behind the Church. Miss Elizabeth Walsh was one of the earliest, if not the first Headmistress.

The school was built to accommodate 120 children but it was recorded that in the first year the average attendance was only 86. The first Teacher recorded (in 1867) was Miss Ellen Hayes, and in 1870 she was advised the school would have to close, *"as the Mission was too poor to pay a teacher"*, but this did not happen, although in the early years there appear to have been frequent changes in the teaching staff. For example, Nora Buckley took charge of the school on 10 January 1881, a certificated mistress from Wandsworth Training College. There were then 78 children and only ten of these were Catholics. She left in October 1882 and subsequently married Mr W. Barnes. Then followed Miss Catherine Higgins, Mary Elizabeth Savin and Miss J. Boyle. During this time, in 1883, a mistress was given a month's notice for declining to assist in the Church Choir! In March of 1884 Miss Buckley returned as   Mrs Barnes to take over the school until 1888 when Miss Elizabeth Courtney became Head.

Children were taught the basic 3R's and to sing and recite as well as being nurtured in the Roman Catholic faith. The priest in charge of the Mission was always a regular visitor to school and watched the children's progress with interest. In the early days, he and wealthy members of the town often brought "treats", sweets and fruit for the children and sometimes supplied teaching materials in the form of framed slates and books.

As in all the schools in early years, the senior pupils became pupil teachers and often followed on to become teachers in their own right. Drawing wasn't introduced until 1891 and was never given the prominence of needlework which took up Wednesday and Friday afternoons. School hours were from 9.30 - noon and 1.45 - 4.00 p.m., and on Monday mornings the children were expected to bring their school fees for the week's tuition. For Senior pupils, Standard IV and above the rate was threepence and for Juniors and Infants two pence. However, such was the poverty that fees were often *"badly paid"* and were occasionally met by the Poor Law Guardians. When enlargement of the Church in 1890 was delayed by the death of the contractor the church services were held in the large room over the schools until completion in 1892.

Holidays were always granted for traditional Poole Fair Days and when the Circus came to town, and of course on occasions of Royal Celebrations such as Coronation Day. The children in the early days were not classed by age but according to classified standards and children of weak intellect or delicate health were withheld from exams and did not "move up". At one time a third of the school were on this "Exception Schedule"; not surprising really when it is recorded that newly admitted sisters aged 9 and 10 knew nothing, not even the alphabet! Ailments were rife, and these included chickenpox, measles, mumps, diphtheria and tuberculosis. When one of the babies, aged 3½, died of Scarlet Fever, the entire school was scrubbed and disinfected throughout with Jeyes' Fluid.

But things moved on; the school was extended to accommodate 200 pupils and average attendance grew to 130. The upper classroom, used by the senior children measured 31ft 4ins by 17ft and 13ft 1ins high. The Infants room was 24ft by 19ft 3ins with a height of 14ft 6ins. Each classroom had a coal fire guarded by a substantial fireguard. In the years that milk was delivered to school in one-third pint bottles for free distribution to the children, old pupils remember the bottles being lined up round the fireguard during the cold winter months to take off the chill before drinking it at playtime.

Although the school was mixed, at playtime a fence across the play area separated the sexes. The toilets were outside and washing facilities merely a sink under the stairs. The school continued much the same during the First World War, a Miss McFaul being a driving force behind the Infants. She lived on the doorstep, so to speak, in a house in Market Street just along from the Police Station. The companion who shared her house was a teacher of music to many children of Poole.

The substantial floods of the winter 1924 swamped much of the lower town and caused disruption to school attendance. In 1933 Miss O'Regan resigned and her place was taken by Miss Catherine Twomey. Then just before World War II the school was classified as a **Junior Mixed and Infants' School.** There were no Air Raid Shelters and the children remember holding tin trays over their heads when the sirens sounded as they made their way into the presumed safety of the church.

It was not until June of 1943 that a telephone was installed. School dinners, delivered from Henry Harbin School's kitchens were served for the first time in 1945. The condition of the school left much to be desired – outside toilets, no hot water, no staff room and coal fires that smoked.

In 1949 Miss E. Cassidy took over as Head from Miss Hussin, who had been Headmistress since 1921. As Sister Gabriel, Miss Cassidy reigned supreme until Sister Anne Joseph became Head in September 1979. Mrs Randall, who had joined the staff in 1949 became Deputy Head in 1951 and remained in that post until her retirement in 1981. The school overflowed into the Church Hall and nearly all the children at the school were Catholics.

In 1958 Lagland Street School accommodated the St Mary's remedial children and the Oddfellows' Hall at Hunger Hill was used for school dinners in addition to supplying another much-needed classroom. In the early 60's, with the number of children increasing, four classes were transferred to Lagland Street.

In 1965 the much needed replacement school at Devon Road was opened and the old school closed. Sister Anne Joseph remained in charge until she retired in July 1995. A new Head, Mr Maurice O'Brien took up his duties in January 1996.

1970 – Headmistress Sister Gabriel and teacher Sister Aidan joining in the fun at the Devon Road School Fete.

*1913 – The entire school drilling outside the new premises.
Mr. Prankard and Mr. Smith in background.*

*1912 – Mr. Prankard and his class posing proudly to show their new desks and chair in the
brand new classroom.*

South Road School

The new Elementary Schools erected in South Road, Poole, were formally opened on Friday afternoon, 5th January 1912. The opening ceremony was carried out by the Mayor, Councillor J. A. Hawkes, amid an impressive gathering of leading townsfolk and churchmen.

The school was erected by the Borough Council using its powers as local education authority. The British Schools had been told to improve their premises, but had been unable to do so and recognition was to be withdrawn. There was an urgent need to find alternative places. The proposals were also opposed by the National School Managers as they realised their own school opposite would be threatened, but the Board of Education gave the South Road Schools approval.

The school building looked then as it does today, but without the extensions built on the front, and the side play areas. It was situated on about an acre of land, bought from Mr J. J. Norton for £1,500, forming a portion of the site of the Lewin Iron Foundry between South Road and Green Road. The accommodation was for 290 boys and 290 girls, a total of 580 children. The Boys' entrance was from South Road and the Girls' from Green Road, the latter occupying the classrooms on the first floor only. The exterior was built of South Western Pottery white-faced bricks with terracotta dressings by Messrs Carter and Company. The roof was tiled. Both sections of the school consisted of five classrooms, cloakroom accommodation, lavatories of the latest pattern, also a teacher's room, store room and other conveniences. The first floor, which was reserved as the Girls' department, was approached by a wide staircase of granolithic material. In each of the schools three of the classrooms were arranged so they could be thrown into one by the drawing back of folding partitions. The classrooms were all fitted with dual desks. Throughout was a glazed tiled dado, and the walls above were coloured light green. The floors were of maple wood blocks, the heating was on the low pressure hot water system and was carried out by Mr Haydon of Trowbridge. The schools were extremely well lit with large windows. The electric lighting had been installed by Mr A.G. Strudwicke of Branksome. The first floor was of fireproof construction of Messrs Homan & Rogers' patent, and outside a fire escape staircase was provided. The playgrounds were tar paved and contained playing sheds for the shelter of children in wet weather. The site was surrounded by iron railings set in a stone coping. The erection at the time had been carried out practically without extras being incurred, the contract price had been £6,780 and the furnishings had cost about £350 making a total of £7,130. The schools had been built by Mr H. W. King of Springbourne from designs by the Borough Surveyor, Mr S.J. Newman.

There was a large attendance at the opening ceremony over which Mr G. C. A. Kentish, Chairman of the Education Committee, presided. In addition to the Mayor, who was accompanied by the Mayoress (Mrs. J. A. Hawkes), the Company also included the Sheriff, many Aldermen, Councillors, the Town Clerk (Mr C. Lisby), the Borough Surveyor, the Medical Inspector of Schools, the Rector of Poole (Reverend H. Lawrence Phillips), and many of the leading Churchmen from the various churches and chapels in the area. Mention was made of those present, Alderman George Curtis, Mr J. W. Buckley and others who had been connected with the Voluntary School Movement for a number of years, and they were heartily thanked them for the splendid services they had rendered. The Mayor said he was sure all would rejoice at the town possessing such splendidly equipped schools as were being opened that afternoon. The Mayor then referred to the fact that the premises which had been vacated (the British School) were now free for Sunday School work, and went on to say that in 1904 the numbers of scholars nationally in Non Provided Schools and the Council Schools were almost identical but last year (1911), although there had been an addition of a million more scholars, there had been a decrease in the Voluntary Schools of something like 25,000 scholars with 300 less schools. Those who had favoured the Voluntary system might feel depressed, but it was agreed that whatever system they supported the very best should be provided for their children. At the end of the Mayor's speech, Mr Reynish who had been for many years Headmaster at the British School, proposed the vote of thanks to the Mayor and the Chairman. When the ceremony was over, the schools were inspected by all present and tea was served through the hospitality of the Mayor.

The Heads of the Old British School in Lagland Street, James Reynish and Edith Lowe, took over the Headships of the new South Road Schools, but Mr Reynish to whom, upon the recommendation of the Education Committee an extension of two years' service had been granted, was not in the best of health, and in June 1913 Mr J. W. Prankard took over as Head of the Boys' Section. His Headship lasted until May of 1926 when Harry Peace Smith took over until the advent of Henry Harbin School in 1939 where he became the first Headmaster. Miss Edith Lowe was superseded by Miss E. J. Jeffery who reigned supreme as the Girls' Head until the new Henry Harbin Senior School was built in 1939. Miss G. M. Harding (of St James') was the first Headmistress of that school. From 1939 onwards, South Road Junior Council Mixed School for pupils up to eleven years of age, had only Headmasters the first of whom was Mr A. J. Martin from the National School – (3rd April 1939 to 31st January 1942).

Mr James Reynish had 220 boys on his register at the opening of the new **South Road Boys' School** in 1912. These boys were aged between 6 and 14 years of age, and had been accepted from the British, St Paul's, St James', and private schools in the area. One of his first duties was to hand out five pairs of boots to really needy boys. It was not unknown for boys of large families to walk barefoot to school carrying their boots around their necks, to wear them all day in school and then take them off and carry them on the journey home, to extend the life of the boots so that they could be handed down, probably many times, before eventually being discarded.

The staff and pupils were proud of their purpose built school and playground, which they enhanced by the digging of a border under the windows in which to plant shrubs and flowers. Soon after the opening, on 26th January, a load of earth was delivered to school for this purpose, and at the end of March planting of shrubs took place followed a month later by the sowing of flower seeds.

Three months later, Mr Reynish reported that the six dozen school caps ordered for the boys were not to hand, but certificates, paints and books were distributed by way of reward for good work and attendances. For reasons not stated, Mr Kentish, Chairman of the Education Committee, and the Borough Surveyor visited the school on 15th March and decided that the flagstaff, which had been erected only one month previously, was to be removed. One assumes that this was just for a change of position, for the flagstaff played quite an important role in the school life, especially on occasions such as Trafalgar Day, May Day, and royal events.

An event disturbing both for Mr Reynish, his staff and the boys, occurred on the first Monday in May when on dismissing the school at 4.20 p.m Mr Reynish was distressed to see a soldier half hanging out of a window overlooking the school yard. This window was in the adjacent Drill Hall, and at first the Headmaster thought he had fallen through the window in a faint and cut himself, for blood was flowing copiously down the wall. However, it was proved later that the man had shot himself in the head. The boys were late home that day for they were kept in until the body had been removed.

At the opening of school for the autumn term, 28 infants were admitted from the British Infants' School, 4 from St Paul's, 5 from St James', and 2 from private schools, making the number of boys now 243. Arithmetic was given such a prominent place in the school curriculum, that in December Mr Irving, HM Inspector, refused to approve the timetable on the grounds that too much time was devoted to arithmetic.

The age breakdown at the end of 1912, after pupils holding Age Certificates had been allowed to leave, was as follows:-

Between the ages of six and seven	6 Pupils.
Between the ages of eight and eleven	132 Pupils.
Between the ages of eleven and fourteen	83 Pupils.

Mr Reynish was a very sick man indeed, and although he was granted leave of absence in January 1913 to go for a change of air to hasten his cure, by March the Headship was being advertised and applications were invited. Although Mr Reynish wrote a Testimonial to support Mr Townsend's application, it was Mr J. W. Prankard of Oakdale School and formerly a pupil teacher at Poole British School, who succeeded as Headmaster on 9th June

1913 – Miss Perry with her class at their new dual desks.

1913. (Mr Townsend went as Headmaster to Oakdale School). The staff were:- Harry Tandy, H. P. Smith, T. E. Glover, B. Wight , Miss Perry and Miss Cooper.

Mr J. W. Prankard was the personification of the contemporary idea of the "grand old type" Headmaster. He was not very tall, about 5'6", with grey, wiry hair, he lived in Fernside Road opposite what is now the Municipal Buildings. In those days it used to be called Brown Bottom. He was married, and his wife had a very exclusive dress shop in the High Street, just below the level-crossing gates, called Madame Prankards, this was later to become Boulds Gown Shop (now a Superdrug store).

Madame Prankard was later to move to other premises opposite the Post Office. In his spare time, Mr Prankard used to help voluntarily at the Cornelia Hospital. X-Ray was in its pioneering days, and he spent hours helping to work the X-Ray machine. At that time the dangers were not known, but he developed a paralysis on the left side of his face which most people took to be the effects of a slight stroke, but in effect it was the radiation that caused it, and had badly affected his speech. In spite of this, he was a marvellous story teller, and the pupils of the time vividly remember his *Westward Ho*, his Dickens, and his *Lorna Doone*.

One of the first duties he performed as Head was to set the boys to practice Fire Drill, and in 50 seconds they cleared the building, witnessed by Mr Kentish, Chairman of the Education Committee, and Colonel Lawrence.

On an equally serious note, a revised booklet published by order of the Education Committee was issued to the Headmaster of South Road School, and indeed to all schools in the Borough, for the guidance of Managers and teachers regarding Infectious Diseases. This booklet set out in great detail the course of action to be followed for the fevers, diseases, and verminous conditions, as well as tuberculosis or consumption, which prevailed at the time.

Mr H. P. Smith, who was to become the next Head in 1926, transferred to South Road as a certificated assistant from Courthill School in July 1913, and in December of that year Mr B. Wight resigned and received a leather pocket wallet as a gift.

The First World War was looming, and as the Drill Hall was situated next to the school, the boys' playground was used periodically for assembling the volunteers who had been recruited from local pubs and meetings. They were paraded, still in their ordinary civilian clothes, to the accompaniment of the Town Band, or a Military Band, as far as Poole Station where they were taken by train to Dorchester Barracks. Crowds of friends and relations would follow them along the road in order to give them a really warm send-off.

The school syllabus in 1914 comprised Physical Training, Language Training (reading, recitation and composition), arithmetic, geography, history, and nature knowledge and woodwork. The models for this latter subject were varied, and for the most part quite innocuous. To name but a few, a wall bracket, flower support, a wicker gate ink-stand, a sink tray, and a match-box bracelet. Until we learn that wood had been received to make two desks for defectives ! So great was the interest shown in the woodwork classes since their inception in October 1913, that by February a separate show-case at the Museum in Mount Street had been set aside to house some of the woodwork models. These woodwork classes were at that time held in the corridor, and before each lesson the six benches, each of which accommodated four boys, had to be carried in to school from the store where they were kept. At first the tools the boys used were not very satisfactory, and the equipment was insufficient for the number of pupils. However, after visits by Woodwork Inspectors, this situation was rectified and the boys eventually received two dozen saws (large and small), 18 hammers, 18 bradawls, and a tool cupboard.

When the new school year commenced on 1st April 1914, Mr Prankard welcomed 27 new infants, and promoted the existing scholars, immediately before Prayers. He seemed a little disappointed in the standards, for he wrote, *"Younger boys lean too much over their desks, often in dirty clothes, and untidy. Walls to the sanitary offices are dirty and need more frequent lime washes"*. No wonder then that an epidemic of diphtheria broke out shortly after school started, and not only children who were suffering from this disease, but also those whose families were affected, were excluded from the school. Less than a year later one of the staff, Mr T. E. Glover, was ordered from the school by the Ministry of Health having entertained soldiers who were subsequently found to have been suffering from scarlet fever.

A member of the staff, Mr Harry Tandy, left school on 9th September having joined the Army, (the Town Clerk had agreed to continue paying his salary less army pay and emoluments and hold his position open until the end of hostilities) and the caretaker left to act as guard over German prisoners at Dorchester. Other members of staff who were at later dates called for Military Service were Mr Lydford, T. E. Glover, R. O'Brien, and the same salary conditions applied.

November was a very sad month, Mr Reynish (the previous Headmaster) died and was buried at Parkstone Cemetery on 5th November. On the 18th November the lads were marched up to the tram terminus to pay their last token of respect to a Belgian soldier who had died of wounds.

The first intimation of the influence that Mr H. P. Smith, was to have on the school and indeed on Poole, came in June 1915 when a party of senior boys visited Badbury Rings one evening to view the magnificent earth works. Much, much more was to follow but this was the first glimpse.

Three boys gained scholarships to the Poole Secondary Grammar School this year, one of whom, C. Lee Hartnell, was to become Headmaster of South Road 1945-1964.

By September, evening continuation classes commenced and in order that the War Regulations regarding the "Black-Out" were met Messrs Butler were called in to make sure all the window blinds were adequate.

1916 started cold and snowy and attendances were very low. The student teacher, Raymond O'Brien, received permission from the Town Clerk (Charles Lisby) to enrol in the 9th Hants (T). On the 7th June it was the Headmaster's sad duty to announce to the boys the loss at sea of Lord Kitchener and his staff. The flag in the playground was flown at half-mast.

The local places of worship had not completely lost contact with their flock, for during the summer they invited the children to spend half a day being taken to a local beauty spot, having tea provided and perhaps organising a few games and prizes. In deference to these occasions, half-day holidays were granted during the summer months of June and July by the school.

By September Mr Smith was required to attend the Medical Board at Dorchester for examination in response to his army call. However, he was passed for sedentary work at home only. On return to school in November after the autumn break, attendance was low, measles and colds were prevalent. In addition, extraordinarly violent south-west gales had brought severe flooding to some of the homes of the boys. Clothes had become sodden. The woodwork lessons at school suffered as the rain was far too severe for the benches to be brought in, and in any event, corridors where woodwork was carried out were so dark that the boys would not have been able to have seen what they were doing.

In spite of all these local difficulties, a War Savings Association was formed in conjunction with the girls' and infants' departments, and in December the children collected ten shillings to send to the soldiers' fund of the Weekly Dispatch, and fifteen shillings and three pence to the Overseas Club Fund for Soldiers.

Mr. Smith with class 2 boys — 1914.

Parents of the boys were asked to make application if they required an allotment, and to specify the amount of seed potatoes they would wish ordered for them, and by the beginning of 1917 a considerable number of replies had been received requesting same.

Bad weather got worse and heavy snow caused the school to close for a day early in March. The attendance when school opened again was very low and an epidemic of mumps was prevalent.

Sgt Tandy however visited the school and was pleased to announce that he had been granted a commission. The boys seem to have hobbled through 1917 dogged by bad weather and the war, but nothing dampened ardour on 24th May, Empire Day, and the great deal of pomp and ceremony that was always attached to that. The flag was saluted by the boys formed in the hollow square in the playground. The National Anthem was sung and a special lesson given. The afternoon was, as always, made a half-day holiday.

1918 started with a very poor attendance, the reason given being the fact that the shops started selling margarine and other goods in short supply at 10 o'clock and parents were keeping the children from school to take charge at home, whilst they waited in the queues. There was an epidemic of ringworm, mumps and measles as well. Maybe it was fortunate that attendance was so low, as the classes had to be grouped together in order to release some of the teachers to assist the local food control committee, working from the gymnasium in Mount Street. New ration books were in the process of being issued, and teachers were required for clerical work in conjunction with this.

The WSA team seem to have really taken off the ground for on 19th June the children were granted a day's holiday for "Children's Tank Day". On this day children who belonged to the WSA marched from their respective

1923/4 – Master 'Bonny' Haines with group 9 boys in playground. Names recalled: Brett, Tanner, Nuttal, Smith, Ingram, Baker, Wells, Jenkins, Goff, Dearden, Willis, Elsden, Golding, Padley, Wallingford, Rabbetts, Francis, Long.

schools to Poole Park to view the visiting tank, purchase additional Certificates and listen to an address from the Mayor. As the total savings at the South Road Boys' Department for that week amounted to £205.11s.0d, one assumes that the occasion was a creditable success. The War was drawing to its end. Although school reopened on the morning of 11th November after a three week enforced break on account of a flu outbreak, the afternoon was given as a holiday in celebration of the Armistice.

Mr Prankard was a sick man. On 13th December the Managers authorised his absence until after the Christmas holidays to enable him to enter a Bournemouth Nursing Home. In his absence H.P. Smith allowed some 60 boys to start and finish half an hour early on Wednesday before the Christmas break so that they could attend a party at the Congregational Church, Lagland Street. Mr Prankard was not well enough to return to school after the Christmas break but by 3rd February 1919 he was back in command. Mr Smith had gone to Leicestershire to attend his mother's funeral. Mr Lydford had returned to school duty having been discharged from the Army where he had secured a Commission. He was to serve at South Road for only a short time for he was transferred to the National School on 22nd September and was presented with a walking stick on the occasion. Mr Tandy was to return later in the month on 24th February after demobilisation.

A most important new building – the Dr. Barnardo's Nautical Home (Russell Cotes) – was being built on the slopes of Constitution Hill, and the visit of His Royal Highness Prince Albert to Poole to lay the Foundation Stone of this building on 8th May 1919 was cause for the granting of a day's holiday. An important event which always earned a half day holiday was Empire Day, 24th May. The fact that it fell on a Saturday or Sunday made no difference for in that case the event was celebrated on the Friday before, or the Monday after, in the presence of the Chairman of the Governors, (Alderman J. A. Hawkes in 1919), the School Managers (Messrs Buckley, Bollam and Green in 1919), and some parents.

The annual Arts and Crafts Exhibition held at Dorchester this year brought recognition to the school which was commended, and for pupils Sims and Dawe who were awarded Certificates for their pastel, brush and pencil drawings.

18th July was given as a holiday to enable the Peace Celebrations to take place, and a tea party was organised for the children.

On the Railways it was not peace but strikes, and this delayed the newly appointed Certificated Assistant, Mr C. J. Thomas (who was to stay at South Road for less than one year) from taking up his post from the 3rd to 6th October. He was replacing Mr H. P. Smith who had left on 5th September to take up a new appointment at the Technical School, Portsmouth. A presentation of a solid leather case had been made to him from the Staff and Scholars on his departure.

School premises were used on 31st October for the No. 2 Ward Municipal elections which necessitated the granting of another day's holiday, and before school closed for the Christmas break that year impetigo, ringworm and influenza had a markedly low effect on attendances. At the beginning of the new year, 1920, the Medical Officer of Health issued pamphlets on the "Prevention and Treatment of Influenza" for distribution to the scholars to take home for their parents' perusal, and then for three days in February Dr. Nankiwell (the Medical Officer of Health) came to the school to examine the scholars.

But, as in the previous year, 1920 started with a death in the family of a member of staff. Mr Tandy's wife died on the morning of 14th January. Ill health necessitated the appointment of a Deputy School Attendance Officer and Mr W. H. Knight of 26, Garland Road took up this duty in the place of Mr E. J. Conway.

The annual June events of the school outings (this year to Weymouth, and senior parties to go forward to Portland, Abbotsbury and Portisham), and the Poole Carnival gave rise to two more days' holiday, and of course in July the school took up its option of four half-days' holiday, as opposed to the alternative of two whole days, which was open to all Elementary Schools in Poole. In addition, for every four week period of attendances over 94% a reward half day was awarded and advised by the Town Clerk. School closed for the summer vacation most of August, and when it resumed at the end of August 1920 Mr Charlie Lee Hartnell commenced duties as a Student Teacher.

Six boys had won seven scholarships. Two with the Dorset County Education Committee (one an Agricultural Scholarship) and five had been granted Junior Scholarships with Poole Education Committee. Those concerned were Eric Houston (DCC Agriculture), Clarence Alexander (Junior DCEC), and Cyril Tapper, Kenneth Sommerton, Willie Read, Willie Selby, and again Eric Houston (Poole Junior EC).

With Mr Thomas leaving the school in September to take up an appointment at Eastleigh, and Miss Compton following suit in October to Nottingham, the staff shortage became acute and Miss Jeffery, the Headmistress of the Girls' School, loaned first one of her teachers Miss Buckmaster, and then another, Miss Arnold, to assist Mr Prankard. He was having to take Standards IV and V combined, and his health was far from good.

However, the contrary conditions seemed not to have impaired the school efforts, for Bert Cluett of the VII, in the face of competition from all scholars attending Elementary schools in the Borough, won First Prize - a silver watch-in an Essay Competition. This competition had been held in conjunction with a film the children had been allowed to view at the Poole Electric Cinema on the morning of 14th September entitled 'With Shackleton to the Antarctic'.

In December 1920, Mr H. P. Smith (Certificated) returned, albeit temporarily in the beginning, with the approval of the Chairman of the Managers and the Town Clerk. During the Christmas recess, Mr Prankard had undergone serious surgery. When school resumed in January 1921, Mrs. L. Cox started duties as an Uncertificated Assistant taking Standard V and Mr Tandy took care of the Log Book in the Headmaster's absence.

This year, new regulations communicated by the Town Clerk came into effect, and a list of boys likely to leave at the end of term was from henceforth to be sent to the Juvenile Employment Committee at the Employment Exchange at the commencement of each term. As a result of this, on 18th March the boys who were leaving, together with their parents, were interviewed at school with regard to their future careers. By this time Mr Prankard had returned to duty, and Councillors Cole and Kendall had now been appointed as School Managers, in addition to Mr J. W. Buckley.

In October forty selected scholars from the senior classes, accompanied by Mrs. Cox and Mr Haines, marched to Ashley Road, Upper Parkstone, to see a film "Christopher Columbus" at the Victory Palace.

1922 saw the start of a Boot Club with the Misses Lindsay acting as Secretary and Treasurer. School followed its usual routine. Terminal Tests were sat and prizes distributed immediately before Easter, Summer and Christmas vacations. These prizes were purchased from the Harbin Trust Fund which was allocated each year and recipients were voted for by the boys in secret ballot.

Empire Day in May and Trafalgar Day in October were always celebrated and half-day holidays given. In addition, during June a day's holiday was

Staff Group 1925 – Back row: Mr. Read, Miss Shepherd, Miss Cooper, Mr Hillier. Seated: Mr. Tandy, Mr. Prankard, (Head) Mr. Haines. Mr. Prankard was in poor health and retired early the following year.

allowed to enable the boys to enter the one day Elementary Schools' Athletic Sports held in Poole Park. Later in June, the Annual Sports of the Dorset County Schools' Athletic Association were held at Dorchester. Poole Carnival, usually held in mid-June, became a day's holiday as such a low attendance had always occurred in the early school days. The two whole days' or four half-days holiday allowed during July to the Elementary Schools were usually taken as four Wednesday afternoons, because Wednesday was early closing day in the town and the children of people working in the shops were able to accompany their parents on various summer afternoon activities. Royal events, Polling days, Football Honours or Girl Guide Rallies, all would qualify for a holiday from school, which was a mixed blessing for some who preferred the comparative comfort and security of their classrooms to what their homes had to offer them.

Scholarships were awarded to seven boys this year, three Agricultural Scholarships tenable at the Grammar School, Beaminster, and four at Poole Secondary School.

Just before school broke up for the summer holidays, the Annual School Outing occurred, and in 1922 this was a Royal Blue charabanc to the New Forest visiting the Rufus Stone and Beaulieu en route. Departure from school at 8.30 a.m. and return at 7 p.m. Route maps were supplied to all.

During the summer holidays the school was thoroughly cleaned and scrubbed, and the corridors and small rooms repainted. In December, the Harbin Trust "Best Boy" Prize was awarded by result of the secret ballot, to

1925/6 South Road Boys with the Poole Borough Schools Trophy. Back row: Ingram, Woolacott, Brett. Middle row: Hussey, Kneller, Baker, Wells, Dear, Marsh, Wallingford. Front row: Mainstone, Elsdon, Padley, Amey.

Reg Home the same boy who had won First prize in the Health Week Competition held throughout the Borough earlier in the month. After the prize distribution, the Managers and guests usually toured the school and partook of tea. However, in 1923, after the December prize distribution, the Managers held a meeting to consider the conduct of the caretakers wife's on the previous Monday afternoon. Whether good or bad or had anything to do with the fact that a deputy caretaker (Mr Marsh of Denmark Road) had reported for duty with written authority from the Council on 30th November, one will never know.

1923 was the year of the Duke of York's wedding on 26th April, and Mr Prankard returned for duties, on half-days' only basis to start with, in June. His continued ill health was having an adverse effect on the school which was reflected in a very poor school report by H. M. Inspectors. The only bright spot was the formation of two football teams which had procured the use of a playing field in the area (Breakheart Lane – now Fernside Road), and the teams were to go forward to bring much honour to the school in the course of the next few years. The first was in the October of 1925 when the South Road Boys' won the Challenge Cup and Shields being Champions for the 1924/25 season. During July 1924, fifty boys and three teachers went to the Wembley Exhibition, in two groups. Miss B. M. Shepherd joined the staff on 31st August 1925 to take the place of Miss Perrin of Standard I.

The end of this year was marred by an epidemic of measles; the condition of the Headmaster also deteriorated. One of his last duties was to send to Dorchester the number of scholars in Junior, Middle and Senior age groups. In January 1926, he tendered his resignation to take effect on 30th April, and in the interim period he spent much time attending for medical treatment in London.

Mr Harry Peace Smith was appointed successor to Mr Prankard, and although he spent many hours familiarising himself with staff and scholars in the days after the Easter break, he was not able to take up his duties permanently until 17th May 1926. HM Inspector C. D. Paule visited school on 20th May and expressed concern at the practice of grouping classes, and the gross overcrowding especially in Standards VI and VII.

Mr Smith took a new broom, and not only introduced a new timetable immediately, but also reallocated the staff and introduced Specialisation by certain masters who were to teach the specialist subject to classes other than their own. The new timetable proved most satisfactory and the school seemed to take on a new lease of life. Mr Smith encouraged expansion of the school library, and monies received back from the Committee responsible for the Wembley Exhibition visit in 1924, and which had proved surplus to requirements (£1. 16. 6d.) were paid into the Library Fund together with the £2.0s.0d. Prize Money received as First Prize winners for the School Tableaux at the Poole Carnival on 14th July with their entry entitled 'Prosperity to Poole'.

On the 1st September 1926 Mr Charlie Lee Hartnell (a former pupil and student teacher) commenced duties and replaced Mr Read who had been accepted as a candidate for the Wesleyan Ministry.

As an educational experiment, Mr Smith had obtained permission from Messrs Carter of the Poole Potteries for the boys from Standard VII to carry out systematic excavations of the meadow at Hamworthy in which Roman and Celtic remains had recently been brought to light. These excavations were to play an increasingly important part of school life, and later the findings were incorporated in his *"History of Poole"*. Mr Smith was also to be responsible for the renovation of Scaplen's Court, the Old Town House at the lower end of High Street, and he was a pioneer voice regarding Poole's right to assume County Borough status.

November seems not to have been the school's most happy month. The 8th November 1926 saw the school flag flying at half-mast to mourn the death of the Chairman of the Managers, Alderman J. A. Hawkes.

Towards the end of November the Town Clerk was sent what was to become an annual return of a list of streets in which boys attending South Road School resided, together with the numbers of boys dwelling in each street.

In the run up to Christmas, the Library Fund benefited from the proceeds of an entertainment. *'An Evening with William Knapp'*, was given by the Headmaster and boys in the Wesleyan Lecture Hall; admission was by ticket at 6d. each. William Knapp was a composer who lived in Poole in the eighteenth century, and had acted as Parish Clerk at St James Church for nearly forty years. The boys, fifty of them, sang some of Mr Knapp's almost forgotten hymn tunes. The Headmaster gave a lecture on *"William Knapp and the Poole of his day"*.

An epidemic of mumps was prevalent in the days before the Christmas holidays, and was still around at the resumption of school in 1927. However by March, most of the boys were sufficiently recovered to enjoy the day's holiday allowed upon the occasion of the opening of the New Poole Bridge. Officially thirty boys had been allocated places to witness the opening ceremony in the charge of one teacher, but in addition Mr E. E. Kendall, one of the School Managers (and great uncle of the author), had arranged for 100 senior boys to go on board the Steam Tug "Talbot" to view the event. The ceremony was performed by the Mayor, Alderman Herbert S. Carter. It was a most important day for Poole.

It was now compulsory for all children who would reach the age of between 11 and 12 years on 31st July to sit the Junior School Examination in early March. These exams, held between 8th and 11th March in 1927, were taken by 40 boys from Standards II, III, IV, and V, of the required age group, plus a further two boys under the age of ten years whose parents requested that they should sit the exam. Ten boys had reached sufficient standard to qualify them to sit for the Competitive Examinations for Junior Scholarships and free places.

Terminal Tests throughout the school were completed, the usual list of likely leavers at the end of term was sent to Miss Whitting at the Juvenile Employment Bureau, and Statistics forwarded to the Town Clerk as to the numbers of boys under 11 years of age on 31st March (127) and those of 11 plus at that date (152). The average number of boys on the school register during the year ending 31st March 1927 was 289.

The staff at this time was:- Headmaster, Mr H. P. Smith- Standard VII; Mr Haines (C)-Standard VI: Mr Tandy (C)-Standard V; Mr Hartnell (C)-Standard IV; Miss Cooper (U)-Standard III; Mr Hillier (U)-Standard II; Miss Shepherd (C)-Standard I. The Specialisations were:- Mr H. P. Smith - History; Mr Haines - Geography; Mr Hartnell - Elementary Science; Mr Hillier and Mr Haines - Physical Training; Mr Tandy and Mr Hartnell - Singing and Miss Cooper - Copywriting..

Mr Smith had introduced the House System into school and the four houses were: LONGSPEE - Blue - *'Each for All'*, MONTACUTE -Green - *'I Serve'*, THOMPSON -Red - *'Ever Onwards'*, JOLLIFFE - Yellow - *'Excelsior'*.

Mr E. E. Kendall, one of the school Managers, donated a House Cup and in 1927 this was presented to the Head Boy of Longspee, A. Kneller, at the prize giving day on 5th May.

The school had taken on a new lease of life, and prizes won by the South Road Boys' at the Elementary Schools' Sports Day on 2nd June were presented at a meeting of all the participating schools held the next day at the

Mr. Hillier with his class. Note the inkwells with sliding brass covers and the blackboard cleaner upturned on the front desk. Biblical stories are well illustrated on the back wall together with the boys artistic efforts.

Great Hall, Ashley Cross, Parkstone. The Mayor presented the prizes and South Road had won the Tug-of-War Shield, the Relay Race Shield, and the Rowing Shield. In addition they already held both Senior and Junior Football League Championships (having won every match) and both A and B teams were expected to reach the finals in the Six-A-Side Football Tournament.

The school outing in 1927 was taken by train. It was to Corfe Castle and Swanage, departing 10.30 a.m. and returning on the 7.33 p.m. from Swanage. That was in July of course, and in October when the Prince of Wales came to Poole Park to lay a wreath on the War Memorial, the boys marched from the Ladies' Walking Field, to the Park to witness the occasion. A day's holiday was awarded on the following Friday in honour of the visit. When Miss Cooper left in November, she was presented with a handbag and a Waterman Fountain Pen, which in view of her interest in copywriting, seemed most appropriate.

The end of term Christmas celebrations this year took the form of the

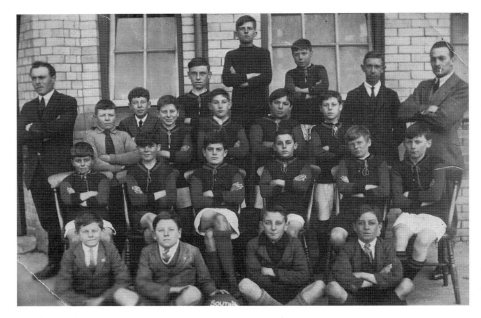

1928 – Mr. Hillier, Mr. Bull and Mr. Haines with the boy's football team. Mr Hillier together with Mr. Bull of Heatherlands School had been responsible for starting the Poole Schools Sports Association.

boys acting Dickens' *"Christmas Carol"* to a paying audience at the Wesleyan Lecture Hall. The performance was repeated at school in front of the boys on the last but one day of term. On that day too, printed Report Forms were used for the first time. These had a tear-off slip along the bottom which had to be returned to the school by the parents, signed to acknowledge receipt. During the Christmas break both Mr Hartnell and Mr Tandy were married.

1928 started with the purchasing of an All Steel 'Adene' Printing Press with the proceeds of the Dickens concert. This the boys worked on resulting in the publication at the end of March of the first volume of a School Magazine, *"South Road Chronicle"*. It was an edition of 28 pages entirely written, illustrated (by means of lino cuts) and printed by the boys of South Road School.

A further acknowledgement of the work carried out by the boys came in May when examples of their printing and lino cuts, together with a portfolio of their work in connection with the excavations at Hamworthy, with actual specimens unearthed, were displayed at the Educational Section of the Agricultural Show at Dorchester. In July, the same exhibition was presented at Salisbury. Much interest must have been aroused for the exhibits were not returned to the school until October, well after the boys had spent their Annual Outing in July visiting Salisbury, Old Sarum and Stonehenge. It is interesting to note that 120 boys and 18 parents went on this outing at a cost per head of 4s.4d., including tea. Another innovation, intimated by the Town Clerk to all schools in the Borough, was that a new term extending from Ist April to 31st May was to be introduced instead of the present arrangement from 31st March to the end of the summer vacation. The school year would in future (as from 1929) start on 1st August and not 1st April.

At the end of October the boys of Standard VII visited a Christmas Exhibition of Sweets organised by Messrs Stickland and Son, Wholesale Confectioners, at their premises in Wimborne Road. The old house adjacent to their warehouse, known as Beech House, was the home of the Stickland family and was built originally for a Newfoundland sea Captain. It afterwards became a small private school run by the Misses Slade. During their visit to the warehouse in 1928, apparently copious notes were taken by the boys and back at school essays were written about their visit.

The start of 1929 brought epidemics of scarlet fever and diphtheria, and heavy snow fell during February. In March the second edition of the *"South Road Chronicle"* appeared and special praise was directed to one of the boys, George Shorto, for his efforts in printing it. Woodwork, which seems to have been overtaken in interest by printing and archaeology, and which had been taken at the Woodwork Centre at Poole Grammar School, took another body blow with the illness of the instructor in April. Woodwork classes were cancelled and for one reason or another they were not resumed until January 1930.

On the sports front the news was all good. South Road first eleven won the Mark Frowde Football Cup against a team from Swanage Council's first eleven in a game played before 3,000 spectators, with three goals scored against nil. The school had won the first round in the Glassey Cup' competition, the Town Shield, and every match in the League games.

For the first time, with the new school year now starting on 1st August, all boys leaving school at the end of July were given a letter by the Chairman of Poole Education Committee, Alderman H. S. Carter, JP. This *'Letter to School Leavers'* contained many words of wisdom and advice to the boys setting out on their first jobs.

The Headmaster, Mr Smith, was granted leave of absence each week to enable him to act as a guide and give a talk to selected scholars from all schools in the Borough at the Old Town House, Poole's first Guildhall. The first of this series of 36 talks was given to the South Road Boys' Standard VII on 4th July.

Mr Prankard the ex-Headmaster of South Road School died at the end of the year, and he was buried on 3rd December. Heavy rain was falling at the time and the lower end of town was seriously flooded.

The year 1930 saw the third volume of the *"South Road Chronicle"* come into being, and the sporting success continued. The Town Clerk, Mr Charles Lisby, informed the school that the alteration to their terms was to continue until further notice. Of the 27 pupils who qualified for and sat the Junior School Examination that year, just two boys, Arthur Burden and Patrick

Jones, were awarded Scholarships to the Grammar School.

Many more boys were beginning to be the proud possessors of a bicycle, and a very daring game had been introduced on the roads. This was to draw behind a passing lorry, and by keeping one hand on the handlebars of the bicycle hold the tailgate of the lorry with the other. Keeping in its slipstream, a very good speed could be maintained. Sometimes two boys would hang on to the back of one lorry, and the danger of one of them falling was very great indeed. But boys will be boys, and the practice continued in spite of the Headmaster bringing in a school rule forbidding this behaviour at the risk of corporal punishment. And so, on 24th September, Fred and James Cartridge, Moore of Standard IV, Samways and Moore of Standard III, and Ridout, all received two strokes of the cane, but the game was too good and well worth the punishment for next day Fred Cartridge, H. Moore and P. Ford had to be caned again. Similar punishment was meted out to Vincent of Standard V and Vick of Standard IV for being caught letting down a cycle tyre in High Street. For swearing, Ford of Standard IV and Cole of Standard I received one stroke.

Mr Tandy returned to school after an absence of eleven months on 29th September, and on 3rd October a presentation of Poole Pottery was made to Miss B. M. Shepherd on the occasion of her marriage on Saturday 4th October. She became Mrs. Kiddle, and the great tragedy was that Mr Kiddle died on the 7th October. (The story was later to have a happy ending when Mrs. Kiddle married Mr Hillier in 1940 - he was then teaching at Henry Harbin). This was the day that John Owen Peace commenced duties as a Certificated Assistant.

The boys kept up their football honours, and this year also saw the Vincent brothers leading the school in the swimming events at the Poole Baths. The Annual Scholarships awarded to lads of the Borough by Carter, Stabler and Adams (Poole Pottery) this year included two South Road boys, F. Mowlem and A. Reed, at first and third places in the examination, and this news was advised to the Headmaster by Mr P. A. Wise of the School of Art, on October 13th. Violin tuition was started, given by Mr Noel V. Hale, LRAM, of Bournemouth, the Principal of Metro Violin Classes. Twelve boys became pupils in the first year, and as these progressed and were able to "show their paces" at the school's Prize Giving day, so the numbers grew until eventually there were three classes; beginners, juniors and seniors.

Another innovation at this time was the swimming lessons conducted each Tuesday morning under the supervision of Mr Hartnell. About twenty boys attended at the Open Air Swimming Baths at the end of Kingland Road (Park Lake Road). Unfortunately, Mr Hartnell contracted diphtheria in September and had to be accommodated at the Isolation Hospital at Alderney. In his absence, his efforts at the Baths were rewarded by E. Vincent winning Councillor Dacombe's Challenge Cup at the Poole Elementary Schools' Swimming Gala.

At the end of June that year the whole school mourned with two of the boys, Roy and Norman Taylor, whose father had been killed in an explosion

1930's Sport's Day at Ladies Walking Field. Some of the participants. Names recalled: Hescroft, Hayes, Biggs.

at the Holton Heath Cordite factory. Not long afterwards, at the beginning of July, Mr Bollam, who had been School Correspondent for so many years, died.

Mr Tandy who had been in ill health for so long applied for a breakdown pension and retired on 31st October after serving for 23 years, first with the British School (he commenced duties there on the 10th September 1908) and then with South Road since its opening in 1912. Shortly afterwards he entered the Royal National Sanatorium at Bournemouth, where Mr Smith visited him on 23rd December to present to him the engraved gold watch from the School Managers, Staff and Scholars.

Another inauguration in 1931 was the supply of milk daily in one-third of a pint sealed cartons. The charge was one penny, to include a straw for ease of drinking. Orders were taken from the boys as class assembled and the milk was delivered at 10 o'clock by Bladen Dairies. It was handed out at 10.25 a.m. just before morning playtime, needy boys receiving the milk free.

The school during 1932 took its customary course, from the January estimates being sent to the Town Clerk for the next year ending 31st March, through the March Preliminary Examinations for Junior Scholarship.

1932/33 – Old Boys Football Club with Trophies. Head H. P. Smith and staff with Jim Philips one of the boys' trainers (R).

Ascension Day holiday was in early May, and a half-day for Empire Day on 23rd May. The year continued through Carnival Day and Poole Elementary Schools' Sports Day in June, and the Annual School Outing in July. Health Week in October, and even November of this year brought its customary sadness, for Lt. Col. F. C. Wheatley, JP, a well loved Poole gentleman and ex Mayor, died. End of term tests, prize giving, visits by the school dentist and the officer from the Juvenile Labour Bureau, the winning of the Glassey Cup again – so the year unfolded, yet not without its changes. The lowest class, as from 1st August was accommodated at Lagland Street School. This was also the year when, in May, the new Municipal Buildings were opened at Park Gates East by the Earl of Shaftesbury. These buildings replaced the premises in Market Street now known as Sir Peter Thompson House.

On 9th January 1933, free meals were given to deserving boys at lunch time at St James Church House. This was started on Tuesdays and Thursdays only, but it almost immediately became a five day a week arrangement.

Building of the hut on the north side of the playground to accommodate two special classes of 'dull and backward' children was commenced during this year, and Mr J.O. Peace encouraged some of the boys to support his great interest in the 3rd Poole Sea Scouts.

The Annual Prize distribution was this year performed by Mrs. Dacombe, wife of the Sheriff of Poole, Councillor A. J. Dacombe.

About this time many childrens' clubs were set up by various film stars, products and the popular press. Many can remember the Ovaltinies, the Mickey Mouse Club, the Shirley Temple Fan Club, or the Bobby Bear Club run by the *Daily Herald*. One of the boys, Leslie Hutton of Standard III, was presented with a Gold Medal for Conspicuous Bravery which had been subscribed for by members of the Bobby Bear Club. This was to acknowledge his action in rescuing a drowning 74 year old gentleman from deep water near the 'bunny' (sluice gates) of Poole Park lake. Hutton, who was only 12, was a member of the Bobby Bear Club.

The magazine '*Teachers World*' agreed to publish a series of twelve full page articles written by senior boys regarding the early Iron Age and Romano-British Settlement at Hamworthy, as revealed by excavations during the past six years. The first of the series was published on 17th May and the payments of thirty shillings per article were used to purchase parts to build an Electric Gramophone for school use.

The old gentleman of 73 years of age, Mr H. G. Tilsed, who had been a cleaner at the school for many years, resigned suddenly on 31st July. A sum of two pounds was collected, and it was intended to make a small presentation to him when school re-assembled at the end of the summer break. Unfortunately he died towards the end of August, and so the two pounds was sent to his widow together with a small wreath.

When school opened again in September, the staff were as follows :- H. P. Smith (Headmaster), H. W. Haines, C. L. Hartnell, J. O. Peace, J. H. Roberts, M. P. Hillier and J. M. Kay. The Managers at the time were Alderman F. J. Bacon, JP, Alderman G. W. Green, JP C.C., Alderman A. Shutler, JP, Mr A. F. Roberts and Mr E. E. Kendall. H. M. Inspectors were P. Lavender, H. L. Burroughs and W. Jewsbury.

By the time the last cheque had been received in payment of the '*Teachers World*' articles, the electric gramophone had been completed under the direction of Mr C. L. Hartnell. A boy called Rockett, of Standard III, together with helpers, had made the loud-speaker cabinet. This was five feet square and had been lined with sawdust to prevent the sound booming. The fret had been cut by L. Hutton in a neat design, embodying the Poole Coat of Arms and a school monogram 'SR'. The fret was painted black, and had been backed by yellow silk to give the school colours. It was hoped that this electric gramophone would play a useful purpose in the Music and English lessons.

Some of the artwork on the historical articles, had been carried out by Peter Witherden and, at the end of 1933, he took first place in the Art Scholarship Examinations held by Carter Stabler and Adams. He was awarded his prize at the Prize Giving Ceremony on 13th October, and on the same evening the Headmaster and boys attended an evening of music by William Knapp, the eighteenth century hymn writer. The programme was attended by Mr D. T. Blandford, also a former Parish Clerk, the great-great-great grandson of William Knapp. Also attending were the Rector, Rev. B. Herklots, and the Curate, Rev. A. H. Davis. The Head Boy at this time was V. Ketchley. He was also a prefect, Captain of the Cricket Team, Captain of the Ist XI Football Team and Class I House Captain of Jolliffe House.

Up to 6th November, milk and biscuits had been provided for necessitous boys at school, but this now ceased and from this day the boys attended Poole Guildhall for free mid-day meals. However, it seemed that some of their parents did not approve of this scheme and the children were not allowed to attend. The idea could not have been a success for on 25th January 1934, the soup kitchen ceased and the necessitous children received once again the milk and wholemeal biscuits as before. By September, free milk was being allocated to about 37 boys and about 100 others were allowed to purchase at half-rate, as many parents were out of work. This meant that about half the pupils on the books were receiving help to some degree.

The swing of the curriculum away from just the three R's to a wider field which had started in the 20's continued, and in the Spring term of 1934 the school was visited by Miss Wintle's Quartet, who played selections from compositions by Mozart. The boys for the most part appreciated these efforts, and later in the term the choir of 40 boys conducted by Mr J. O. Peace performed a musical programme from the psalm tunes of William Knapp. Mr H. P. Smith delivered a lecture and this evening was graced by the presence of the Mayor of Poole All proceeds were put to the 'Knapp Memorial Fund'.

Progress in another direction, thanks to the enterprise of Mr C. L. Hartnell of Standard VI, was the installation of a fine cinematograph. From March 1934 onwards, cinema shows were frequently held in the evenings at school. The films were mainly on loan from various public bodies. For example, one evening in March six films borrowed from the G.P.O. film library were shown.

This cinematograph and the electric gramophone built by the boys were objects of great pride and obviously much interest had been aroused at their homes by talk of these two new acquisitions. In the event the Headmaster arranged for a private demonstration of them to the parents on the evening of the 19th April.

The art work done in conjunction with the *'Teachers World'* articles was also causing a great deal of interest. Letters of appreciation had been received from schools as far afield as Scotland, India and South Africa. Specimens of the boys' art work were sent to both Balliol College and Somerville College, Oxford, for exhibition.

With all these new fields of interest opening up, the Sports and Swimming were far from forgotten. Sports Day in Poole Park and the Swimming Gala held at Poole Baths, and Poole Carnival in June, were still automatically granted a day's holiday. The various Sunday School treats – which quite often were trips to Studland with tea provided, followed by games and sports with small prizes given to the winners – were still acknowledged by the granting of holiday to accommodate them. For example, on 4th July school closed because of Sunday School treats being given by the Salvation Army and the North Street Methodist Sunday Schools.

The school seemed not to put a foot wrong during this period and won swimming honours at the July Gala in the form of both the Junior and Senior Championships and the Team Races.

Most of the Iron Age and Romano-British relics discovered during the last seven years at the Hamworthy site by the senior scholars were mounted, described and illustrated prior to being transported to the Borough Museum, where they were set out for display in a specially allocated room.

When the Medical Officer of Health visited in October to give his annual health talk, the subject was *'The Digestive Processes'*. Normally, next day the scholars were subjected to a competition essay based on the talk, but this year was an exception and instead the competition was artistic. An illustrated motto design based on *'Good health shall be my halo and cleanliness my crown'* was won by Bernard Hawkins.

A sobering influence was brought to bear later in October when Mr J. C. Woolridge of the United Kingdom Band of Hope visited school and addressed the senior boys on the subject of *'Temperance'*.

Having got the main body of the school well and truly occupied, Mr Smith in November turned his attentions to the backward section of 16 boys who had been working in Standard V. For the time being he made himself responsible for teaching them and getting to know their problems.

At the end of 1934 in November the school joined in the rejoicing at the marriage of His Royal Highness Prince George and the Princess Marina, and again in May 1935 at the Royal Silver Jubilee celebrations of King George V, held in Poole Park.

In September, Mr Smith organised an exhibition of the Borough's Charters to celebrate the Centenary of the Municipal Corporations' Act. This exhibition was staged at the Municipal Buildings and the senior boys attended an address in the Council Chamber by Councillor Sir James Marchant.

Even as late as 1936 there were still children suffering from malnutrition, and it was deemed necessary to distribute without charge the one-third pint of milk and one wholemeal biscuit a day to five boys, and the milk and a biscuit twice a day to nineteen boys. However, the boys were on the whole well looked after and well taught at school, and responded alertly to the interest shown in them. When the School Inspector, Mr H. L. Burroughs called in February 1936, he praised the staff and pupils alike. He thought the general conditions of the school were satisfactory but the lack of a Hall and opportunities for games in the playground, were criticised. Domestic subjects were taught at the Centre in Mount Street, and some of the boys received woodwork instruction at the Grammar School. The Cinema apparatus was put to good use for educational films were shown in school hours, and an exhibition on a larger scale given fortnightly in the evening, the proceeds being devoted to extending the work.

The acquisition of the large electric gramophone and a number of records was well repaid by the use made of them during music and English lessons, and the small printing press on which the older boys printed the school notices, concert programmes and the School Magazine, was a great innovation. Wall pictures and decorations executed by the pupils showed considerable merit and full approval was given to the careful card index system by which the progress of each boy was recorded and their later careers noted.

When the autumn term of 1936 commenced, the staff was as follows:-Mr J.O. Peace, Mr C.L. Hartnell, Mr H.W. Haines, Mr J.H. Roberts, Mr M.P. Hillier, Mr J.M. Kay.

Unfortunately the popular woodwork classes were not able to be resumed immediately. The instructor, Mr F.P. Messenger had been involved in a motor accident and was indisposed until April of the following year. Instead, in the autumn term of 1936 the boys found an outlet in constructing a relief map of the bed of Poole Harbour. This had been requested by Alderman H.S. Carter JP CC, Chairman of the Education Committee and was at his personal expense. The boys worked under the supervision of Mr C.L. Hartnell, and the finished relief map was first exhibited on 8th December at a meeting of the Harbour Board. After a plate glass case had been provided, and a suitable inscription affixed, it was presented to the Mayor (also Chairman of the Harbour Commissioners), Alderman Major Mervyn J. Wheatley. He later agreed to its loan for display at the Dorset Arts' and Crafts' 31st Annual Exhibition held at Canford School, where it won a First Class Award.

This map seemed to focus attention on the harbour, for in May 1937 the Education Committee granted the sum of £10.0s.0d. to the Headmaster and Mr Hartnell to make an educational film dealing with Poole Harbour and its industries.

The Stadium, Wimborne Road, was the venue for the Coronation celebrations of King George VI and Queen Elizabeth in May, and all the Poole Elementary Schools attended there in the afternoon and evening of the 13th. Coronation souvenir mugs had previously been presented to the boys at the school by Mr A.F. Roberts, the School Correspondent.

During July of this year, the school annual outing was to Whipsnade Zoo. 138 boys and 6 teachers took the train from Poole to Luton and thence to the Zoo by motor coach. The cost per head, including tea, was 7s.6d.

Sunday School treats still played an important role during the summer months, as holidays were given. Sports Days, too, were eagerly anticipated. Attendance half-day holidays were given and good attendance rated on equal terms with good work on Prize Giving Day. On 22nd December the wife of the Sheriff, Mrs F.C. Reeves, distributed the prizes.

School, around this time, was a hive of activity with Mr Smith always discussing possible future projects as well as his tasks in hand. I think it is fair to say that everyone was delighted when his efforts on behalf of Poole and the School were acknowledged on New Year's Day in January 1938 when His Majesty King George VI conferred upon him Membership of the Order of the British Empire. This award was given for "Services in the cause of Education". The Investiture was held at Buckingham Palace at 10.30 am on

Thursday 17th February, 1938.

In September 1938 the Board of Education, for the first time, acknowledged that the absence of children who were holidaying with their parents during school terms was often unavoidable where places of work closed down during term time. They therefore conceded that for a period not exceeding one week, where this was the case, the scholar should be regarded as attending school and so qualify for an attendance mark.

When Mr Smith once again settled down to school routine, it was the new Henry Harbin School which now claimed a fair amount of his time and attention, with various meetings with the Managers of the new School. They met either on the premises of the new school or at the Municipal Buildings, and as he was responsible for overseeing the equipping of the school as well as interviewing candidates for the appointment of his assistant master, he stretched his resources to the full.

In addition to preparations for this new school, the possibility of war with Germany was already a reality. In February the teachers engaged on a survey of possible available accommodation for evacuee school children from danger zones in the event of a war. In this connection all elementary schools were closed on 11th February, a Friday.

On 28th March, Mr A. F. Roberts visited the school and checked the registers for the last time under the Headmaster, Mr Smith. He bore testimony of the happy relationship existing between staff, managers and the boys, and expressed the hope that the achievements of Mr Smith at the new Senior School would be even more distinguished than those accomplished at South Road.

The number of school terms as from 1st April 1939 was reduced from four to three by the abolition of the mid-autumn term. The result of this decision by the Education Authority was that scholars not exempted by the Education Act of 1936 would be unable to leave school at any time between the date of re-opening of school after the summer holidays and the date of closure for the Christmas holidays.

The Town Clerk had already advised that all scholars who had reached the age of eleven years and upwards on 31st August 1938, should attend the Henry Harbin Senior School, Wimborne Road, at 9 a.m. on Monday, 3rd April 1939.

And so on 29th March the South Road School closed down for two days in order to facilitate transport of furniture and books to the Henry Harbin premises. Mr Smith faced his new task with his customary vigour and optimism, tinged with understandable sadness at leaving behind a school to which he had such an affinity and which marked the end of the all-standard school. His last comments written on 29th March were *"Today therefore is the last day that South Road Boys' School (successor to the Boys' British School) will function as an all-standard school. I should like to set on record my appreciation of the loyal and enthusiastic assistance I have received from the various members of staff, and also of the great interest which the Managers have ever shown in the work of the school."*

The number on the roll at that time was 248 boys.

Of this number, 101 boys who had reached eleven years of age or over on 31st August last were transferred to the new Henry Harbin School. The age breakdown was as follows: - Boys 11+ = 47, Boys 12+ = 39, Boys 13+ = 13, Boys 13+ = 2 eligible to leave at Easter but are remaining

The remaining boys, together with 126 lads transferred from the old National School which was now closed, formed the nucleus of the newly styled South Road Junior Boys' Council School.

1933 – Bobby Bear Club presentation to Leslie Hutton by the sheriff of Poole Alderman Dacombe. Watched by Mr. H.P. Smith, Head. Alderman Green (seated at table) and school managers including, Mrs. Lewis, and Mr. A.O. Roberts.

South Road Junior Boys' Council School

The school opened on 3rd April 1939 with 276 scholars on the roll. These were made up from the junior boys of the South Road school remaining after the seniors had been transferred to the Henry Harbin school, the juniors from the National Boys' School and the Standard I from the Lagland Street Infants' School. The National Boys' brought three of their teachers with them, Mr Martin – who was the new Headmaster of South Road – and Messrs. Beale and Evans. Five of Mr Smith's staff transferred with him to Henry Harbin, and so when the South Road Junior Boys' Council School opened on 3rd April 1939 the staff were: Alfred John Martin (Headmaster), Bertram Beale, Albert George Snook, Samuel Ernest Hooper Lukey. Elizabeth Leonie Dominey (Supply), James McGown Kay and Arthur Griffiths Evans.

In view of conditions which were all too soon to be imposed, the communication received in April from the Board of Education seemed superfluous. They suggested that in the light of modern conditions a maximum of 240 scholars should be taken as the guideline when considering future intakes. However, the boys' department settled in well functioning as a separate entity from the Junior Girls who were housed on the first floor, still under the eagle eye of Miss E.J. Jeffery.

Shortly after term started, preparations for the impending War took up much of the time of the staff who had to attend at the Municipal Buildings for lectures on *Air Raid Precautions At School* and *Treatment of Children During an Air Raid*. Mr. Lukey was instructed to attend gas mask drills, and Messrs. Beale and Evans qualified as Air Raid Wardens. The First Aid Box was replenished by a quantity of bandages, lint and iodine, and even the stationery stock was laid up as for a siege. The Company of E.J. Arnold Ltd., Leeds, was chief supplier of these items.

In June, a room in the Boys' Department was set free for various activities by the taking over of a first floor Girls' Department classroom, and despite all these preparations, it was decided to redecorate the whole of the outside of the school in July.

The summer passed in the time accustomed manner, with the Sports Day, Swimming Gala, Carnival Day and Sunday School treats still highlighted. Blackboards were reblacked, and five boys passed the examinations for free entry to Poole Grammar School in September.

However, before that term was due to start World War II was declared, and reopening of the school was delayed until the 20th September.

As there had been no trenches or shelters constructed at the South Road premises, the school was closed. Some desks and stock were locked away in the two store rooms. Members of staff were aided in this by the Military as the building was now to be taken over temporarily by the War Office. The pianos and many desks and stock were transferred to the new Henry Harbin School where schooling first took place for one session each day only from 1.00 p.m. to 4.30 p.m. To alleviate overcrowding, and to cut out unnecessary travel, children living at Hamworthy were instructed to attend Hamworthy School.

By October, with the children settling in as well as possible in the Henry Harbin building, the schooling reverted to two sessions daily – mornings 9.00 a.m. to 12.00 noon, and afternoons 1.30 p.m. to 3.45 p.m. Three South Road classes were accommodated in the Hall, two in one classroom upstairs and one in another classroom. About 100 boys stayed at the school for a mid-day meal. As though there was not enough dislocation, an epidemic of diphtheria broke out and several of the lads were sent to the Isolation Hospital; one boy, James Cobbam, died. The classrooms had to be throughly disinfected, and many boys thereafter attended at the School Clinic for immunisation.

After Miss E. J. Jeffery, Head of the Girls' Department, resigned in November, the two Departments amalgamated under the Headship of Mr. A. J. Martin, and as from 1st January 1940 South Road once again changed its format and became the South Road Junior Mixed School.

South Road Girls' Council School

From the date of its inception as a full standard school in 1912 to April 1939, the Girls' Department was housed separately on the first floor of the South Road building, and the girls' entrance was from the Green Road side of the school, whereas the boys used the South Road entrance.

Miss Edith Lowe came from the British School as the first Headmistress, but it was Miss Eva J. Jeffery who took over in 1913 and reigned supreme there until April 1939. She remained Head of the Girls' School when it then changed its format to South Road Junior Girls' Council School accommodating girls up to the age of eleven years only. At this age they passed to either the Girls' Grammar or a Secondary Modern School.

It became evident when the outbreak of war in September 1939 necessitated the housing of South Road School in the newly opened Henry Harbin School premises, that Miss Jeffery found the situation a strain. She was now of retiring age, and this she did in November 1939. After that Christmas vacation, the girls' department was no longer a separate section, for the school became South Road Junior Mixed School from 1st January, 1940.

In 1913 Miss Jeffery was a teacher to be feared and obeyed. She stood only about 5' 4", was slim, with her hair looped down over each ear and then back in a bun roll. She ruled with a rod of iron. Pupils and staff who were her contemporaries still shudder at the mention of her name. One thing is certain, she devoted her life to the school, and always had the education and well-being of her pupils entirely at heart. Baptist in inclination, she was a devout member of that choir and she lived in Emerson Road, right opposite the school. She shared the house with her aunt, Miss Wilkins. Mr Wilkins had been a librarian at the Mount Street Library, who met with an untimely end when he was found hanging from the rafters of the adjoining Gymnasium. This Gymnasium also had happier associations with South Road School for it was often used for the practice of Country Dancing routines in preparation for the annual Bovington Country Dancing Festival.

It was Miss Jeffrey's practice at the beginning of each new school year to inspect personally the writing and work of every girl in her school. Schools in those days concentrated on Reading, Arithmetic, Composition and Recitations by heart. Geography and History were also taught, and Singing and Nature Study also appeared on the curriculum.

The day always commenced with Prayers and Scripture. A lesson in Arithmetic invariably started with the children chanting their 'times tables' en

1912 Girls playground. Miss Lowe (Head) (R). Miss Jeffery (L) in gown. Vera Whittaker, author's mother stands 2nd row, 3rd left. Other names recalled: Gertie Davis, Gladys Cartridge, Gladys Habgood, Maud Power, Gwyneth Jones, Ivy Curtis, Doris Primmer, Nellie Shines, Ethel Cave, Annie Barlett, Annie Brown, Winnie Duncan, E. Dyke, N. Jeans.

masse, and if the lesson was English, it was not uncommon for Miss Jeffery to enter the classroom and take over the lessons for a few minutes, chalking on the blackboard words which she considered were commonly mis-spelt and emphasising the letters where the mistakes usually occurred. No one who ever went to South Road School could ever spell 'oCCasion' or 'neCeSSary' wrongly!

The writing was taught on double-lined books, and each letter whether small or capital had to be just so high (or low) and no more. If a mistake was made in spelling or punctuation, or a wrong answer was given to a question, it was not unusual for the offender to be set 100, 200, or even 300 lines which meant that the correction was to be written out the set number of times.

The same precision applied in the needlework lesson where every stitch, tuck or gather had to be correct or it would have to be picked out.

The girls were taught quite advanced four-needle knitting and embroidery. They took great pride in their work and just before the annual Dorset Arts' and Crafts' Exhibition each year extra time was allowed to the girls whose work was to be exhibited. While they were working on the garments they periodically rinsed their hands in a bucket of water which was kept in the classroom for this purpose.

During the First World War the highlights of school life became May

Day with dancing round the Maypole, Empire Day when the Union Flag was saluted by all and patriotic songs were sung; each child received a small flag to parade around the playground. The Sunday School treats which took place every summer consisted of an outing with tea, games and prizes, were always eagerly anticipated, as were the Christmas parties which the children enjoyed each year. At this time the partitions between the three classrooms were pulled back to make a nice big hall. On occasions wealthy members of the community donated small gifts for distribution to the children. Poole Carnival in June was a great occasion, and quite apart from the day itself, the anticipation and procuring of costumes was delightful

By 1921 the staff of Eva J. Jeffery, ACP, LLA was:- R.F.A. Turner (Certificated); C. Pogue (Certificated); E.M. Buckmaster (U); A.Colwill (U); H.E. Clarke (U) and K.F. Arnold (Supply).

The regime was strict, and it would be fair to say that the staff were as much disciplined as the scholars. Play-time was not allowed; it was a case of a break for visiting the toilet and straight back to lessons. The children were taught Shakespeare and practised little sketches from Dickens which were often performed before the assembly at the Christmas parties. As many of the pupils lived in houses with little or no garden, the growing of bulbs was encouraged at school, with competitions to see which class had the most success. In everything they did the children were implored to do better. Miss Jeffery's methods were not always well received by those in authority, and although her good intentions were never in doubt, the remarks made at a later

1912 Teacher Nellie Clark with a class of girls in their new schoolroom. Note the dual desks and ink wells. Names recalled: Cartridge, G. Davies, Dean, Edwards, Keynes.

1913 Smith Road Girls Staff Group. Miss Jeffery (Head), A.C.P., L.L.A. seated centre.

date by HM Inspectors were true of any year at South Road Girls', that this intense concern for progress made for a deal of undue rigidity. Class behaviour was certainly rigid, with no coughing, speaking or undue blowing of the nose. If this was thought to have happened, it resulted either in a slap on the hand with a ruler, standing in the corner of the room, or sitting at one's desk with hands on head for the remainder of the lesson. The bellow *"if you move a hair of your head I'll thrash you"* still rings in the ear of many an old pupil. And it was not unknown for fidgets to be tied into their desks with string!

Despite, or maybe because of all this, there was a strong feeling of pride and honour to belonging to South Road School, and the children worked hard to try to do their best in everything they attempted.

At the beginning of the autumn term in 1922, the daughter of the Superintendent of Schools, Miss Ella Sprackling, commenced duties as an uncertificated assistant.

As had been the case for many years, Health Week was held in October, and during November a General Election meant an extra day's holiday. There was another bonus holiday on 26th April of the following year to celebrate the Duke of York's wedding, preceded three days before by a concert by the scholars to celebrate Shakespeare's birthday.

In June of each year the County Scholarship examinations were sat and Miss Jeffery, when she adjudicated, always *"solemnly declared"* in writing *"that I conducted the examination in a straight forward manner"*.

School years commenced on 1st April when scholars were promoted to their new classes, and then there was always Shakespeare's birthday (23rd April), May Day (1st May) - with dancing around the Maypole, Empire Day (24th May) - an address by Miss Jeffery, patriotic songs and flag waving. School Sports and Oak Apple Day later in May. June brought the County Scholarship Examinations, Poole Carnival, and the Poole Elementary School Sports Day, then followed the school annual outing and Sunday School treats, and so to the summer holidays. A week in October was devoted to Health Week with lectures and competitions, 5th November was Guy Fawkes' Day and the Christmas parties in December were always a highlight. In between times, the school nurse and dentist visited each term, and there was an annual inspection by HM Inspector of Schools; the girls' needlework warranted a separate HM Inspector of Needlework. In 1923 these posts were occupied by Mr. E. J. Walsh and Miss Bowen. Mr. Walsh summed up the position at school when he wrote - *"Headmistress puts high ideals before herself, and Staff and the children."* Various official bodies came to visit and lecture, and after one such occasion the result of the children' essays entitled 'Kindness to Animals' was a first prize and 2 certificates from the Secretary of the RSPCA. Prizes donated from the Harbin Trust monies were distributed at the end of each term for Good Work and Good Attendance.

On 20th January 1925, Miss Edith Lowe, late Mistress of South Road and the British Schools and to whom Miss Jeffery had been assistant, was buried. The school was closed for a half-day in memory.

That same year, on 8th June, Miss Kathleen Rose Penney (whose Mother had acted as a pupil teacher under Miss Rattray) commenced duties at the age of twenty one years. She had passed her Oxford Senior Local examinations with 1st Class Honours in July 1921, had trained at St. Mary's College, Cheltenham, from 1922 to 1924, and had taught for nine months at Sheffield before coming to South Road. Apart from her class teaching she took games and accompanied the contingent of Country Dancers to Bovington each year.

In 1926 a new piano was installed and a great deal of thanks for that was due to the efforts of Mr. Ernest Kendall, one of the School Managers.

1927 was a memorable year for Poole for the new Poole Bridge was opened in March, and in October, His Royal Highness the Prince of Wales visited Poole Park to lay a wreath on the War Memorial.

At school, the first skipping competitions were held, and there was a severe epidemic of mumps to which both scholars and staff alike succumbed. The school continued to receive excellent reports despite the fact that there was a deal of overcrowding, and Miss Jeffery was obliged to take Standard VII from time to time in the corridors, the rest of the time they shared lessons with Standard VI.

Miss Sprackling became Mrs. Beament in 1929 and resigned temporarily, to return later as a Supply Teacher. Many quick changes of staff had taken place over the last few years. For example, Miss Harris started on 1st March 1926 and left on 30th June. Miss Carter commenced on 5th November 1929, and left on 16th May 1930. Miss Williams lasted from 1st October to

December 1930, and Miss Jones from 1st June to 31st August 1931. Miss Wilkinson's course ran from 2nd March to 17th April 1931. The one who stayed on was Miss Wheller, who started as an Uncertificated Assistant on 3rd November 1930.

The Medical Officer of Health about this time was Dr. Horne who visited school periodically, and during the Health Week of 1931 lectured the older girls on the unlikely topic of *'How I Stand Erect'*.

During the dark winter months, afternoon school started earlier to enable the children to get home before darkness fell. Musical appreciation classes were started during the afternoons, and then by the summer of 1934, swimming lessons were in full swing and Hiking Tours were undertaken by some of the girls. Miss Kent from the Grammar School was allowed to come to South Road and give lessons for the experience, but she did not receive any remuneration. The Cookery Classes were held in rooms on the first floor of the Poole School of Art, Mount Street, next to Norton's Free Library.

In 1935 Poole celebrated the Centenary of the Municipal Corporations Act of 1835, and the girls visited the exhibitions and lectures being staged in this connection at the Municipal Buildings, Park Gates. Holidays were given in November of this year to celebrate the wedding of HRH the Duke of Gloucester to Princess Alice, and also to allow the premises to be used for the General Election purposes.

1936 started with the death of His Majesty King George V on 22nd January, and the proclamation of Edward VIII.

Miss Jeffery continued to be a hard task-master, and at times some of the teaching staff grew mildly rebellious. A case in point was when the School Inspector called in 1936 and Miss Penney made sure her class was working after the bell had gone at tea time. When questioned, she said that the children were obliged to stay on until their task was complete. This action reflected in the Inspector's report which read: *"There are now 210 girls in this Department. The Head Mistress teaches the top class consisting at present of 17 girls. As there are six Assistants and but six rooms for the seven classes, two of the classes share a room. Having regard to the status of the teachers and other circumstances, this arrangement need not be challenged. The Head Mistress shows the utmost conscientiousness and devotion in her conduct of the school, and the staff are unremitting in all particulars of their daily duties. Care should be taken however that an intense concern for progress does not make for undue rigidity. The children are so willing and amenable that constant exhortation and reproof are not needed, and they would probably ultimately benefit more by methods of training which provide freedom for self development, and opportunities for the cultivation of initiative, and especially for self reliance. The practice of extending the normal school hours for the correction or completion of exercises by the children is deprecated."*

However, school continued much as usual, through the abdication of Edward VIII in 1936. The newly proclaimed King George VI was crowned in 1937 when much celebration took place, and all the children were presented with a Coronation Souvenir Mug by Mr. Roberts. By the end of

1938 the new Henry Harbin Secondary School was nearly completed.

From 1st April 1939 South Road School ceased to be an all–standard school but catered for children from the ages of 7–11 years only, when they went on either to a Grammar or Secondary School as befitted their academic achievement. Miss Jeffery remained in charge until her retirement in November 1939.

Miss Penney and Miss Wheller were transferred to the new Henry Harbin school and received gifts from the South Road girls. South Road Girls' Council School now became the South Road Girls' Junior School until the 1st January 1940 when the Mixed Junior School came into being.

Folk Dancing Bovington Camp. May 22nd 1937. South Road girls with Miss Penny (L) and Miss Turner (beret) and Miss Wheller (hat) (R). Author, back row – 4th left. Names recalled: B. Norris, M. Moody, M. Green, R. Bosanquet, M. Reeves, L. Joyce, A. Medley, I. Barrington, B. Clark, S. Taylor, Hayes, Galton.

South Road Junior Mixed. 1940 war time group on school steps. Names recalled: Knight, Wellstead, Condon, Honell.

Maypole Day
Photo taken from top of air raid shelter before demolition.

South Road Junior Mixed School

From 1st January 1940 South Road was for the first time a mixed school. Although still housed in the Henry Harbin School, under its Headmaster A. J. Martin, it functioned as a separate entity. The staff under him then were: R. F. A. Turner (Senior Mistress), B. Beale, S. E. H. Lukey, A. G. Snook, J. M. McG. Kay, A. G. Evans, E. M. Buckmaster, I. B. Leake, K. F. Arnold and E. L. Dominey (Supply)

Some of the dual desks and blackboards which were being stored at South Road were transferred to Oakdale and Broadstone schools for use by the evacuee children.

At Henry Harbin School the children and staff adapted well to the adverse conditions, and were praised by the School Inspectors on their visits in February. It was unfortunate that poor Mr Kay dropped a blackboard onto his foot in June and was unable to walk resulting in his absence from teaching for over a month.

Apart from these conditions, very little evidence of the war itself had yet been experienced in Poole, but everyone was prepared. All the windows had been pasted over with strips of paper to avoid as much splintering as possible in case of explosions, and sandbags were stacked everywhere. The childrens' gas masks were frequently examined and had to be carried at all times. If a child arrived at school without his or her gas mask, by instruction from the Ministry of Home Security, he or she must not be allowed into school and would be sent home for it.

Although Poole and district had received its fair share of refugee children, there were still many parents in the area who wanted their children evacuated to America or the Dominions. Wilson Kenyon, the Town Clerk, dealt with these during the summer of 1940.

Air raid warnings had by now become frequent, and after altering the dates of the summer holidays twice it was decided to split the vacation and take it in two parts. All teaching staff were requested to remain in the district during the intervening holiday periods ready for recall at twenty four hours' notice.

Prior to Prize Distribution on 25th July, the children had spent an hour in the shelters after an air raid warning. Air raid warnings came thick and fast. Sometimes the children had spent all night at home in their shelters as bombs were dropped over Poole. After a particularly bad night in August, the school premises at South Road were entered and ransacked by a number of people.

The Coldstream Guards who were using the building were held responsible, and eventually the sum of £118.14.2d. was claimed from the Military Authorities for the missing goods which included the Electric Gramophone and Cyclostyle.

Promotion of scholars was now to take place with effect from 1st August, and on this date in 1940, 51 boys and 32 girls came up from the Lagland Street Infants' School, and 49 boys and 34 girls were promoted to the Henry Harbin School. By the end of August the South Road Juniors were again attending school – still at Henry Harbin premises – only once a day and with the spasmodic attendances, registers were no longer marked.

However everyone rallied to the War Effort. Staff and scholars collected waste paper and scrap metal. Special fund-raising schemes were entered upon and schools vied with each other to send the biggest donations to the many special funds set up; there was the Mayor's Spitfire Fund (£9. 9s 0d. and £1. 3s 9d. to that) and War Weapons Week in November resulted in £140 of National Savings being bought by the South Road scholars towards the Poole Schools' target of £300.

The help of staff was also enlisted for work in the Food Control Offices during afternoons when they were not teaching, and then despite all the trials that the war had brought to the school, Christmas was celebrated in the usual manner with the childrens' party being held at lunch time instead of late afternoon or evening.

The start of 1941 seemed clouded with despondency on all sides. School resumed for a few days and was then closed when a delayed action bomb was dropped in close proximity. It was not until after the Royal Engineers had made it safe at 4.30 p.m. on 10th January that the children were allowed back to school.

Air raid warnings were frequent and a particularly long one from 6.20 p.m. on the 16th through to 5.30 a.m. on the 17th, was made more frightful on account of a severe snow-storm. Absenteeism was no longer an offence; in fact during early February the school was closed officially for a day whilst the heating apparatus was repaired. Its breakdown had caused the temperature in the classrooms to fall well below 40°F.

Many of the girls, and a few of the boys, toiled at the task of supplying HM Forces with knitted comforts. Sometimes a note was slipped in with the parcels. It was in response to one of these that a letter dated 22nd March 1941 was received at school from the Captain of *HMS London*, acknowledging a parcel of sea boot stockings and pullovers. The letter read as follows, *"The splendid comforts which you have made arrived safely in this fine ship which bears such a proud name. Your gifts are very much appreciated by the lucky men who wear them. On their behalf I want to thank you and any friends who helped you for your kindness, generosity and hard work. I should much preferred to have written a separate letter to each donor but the number of gifts we have received and the pressure of work preparing to meet the King's enemies prevents this. Yours sincerely, R. M. Servars, Capt. RN"*.

That school year soldiered on with the teaching staff and scholars attempting as near as possible the normal routine. Efforts on behalf of the Air Raid Distress Fund, Poole Warship Week, and the National Savings Group helped to keep the childrens' interest, and the Headmaster was pleased to learn in August that 12 of his pupils had passed the Grammar School Entrance Examination, where they started in September.

During the time that the South Road scholars had been housed at the Henry Harbin building, a shelter had been erected in the playground of South Road and another at the Lagland Street School. The Military by now had no further use for the building, and so on 26th January 1942 two classes, 1a and 1b, resumed full time attendance at the South Road School building.

To their great disappointment, they found the classrooms and furniture left in a very dirty condition. It was freezing cold because the stoke hole was flooded and there was no heating. There was no alternative but to send the children back to Henry Harbin School again whilst South Road was thoroughly cleaned out. Mr S. Miles of Rothesay, Linden Road, Parkstone, was appointed temporarily as full time caretaker of South Road School at £130 per annum plus a war bonus of eleven shillings per week.

The Headmaster, Mr A. J. Martin, reached retirement age and resigned his post on 31st January, 1942. It must have been a great disappointment to him that the whole of his Headship had been carried out in the premises of another school.

His successor, Mr J. O. Peace, commenced duties as Head on 2nd February, and once again two classes Ia and Ib went back to the newly cleaned, scrubbed and polished South Road premises. There was still no heating, but the children worked full days from 9 a.m. to 12 noon and 1.30 p.m. to 3.45 p.m. It was necessary to establish a rota for the teaching staff who had now to divide their time between South Road and the classes still housed at Henry Harbin.

Eventually the severe cold weather passed, and work was started on the redecorating the outside of the South Road building, and also of extending the air raid shelters in readiness for the return of all the pupils to their own school. In April stock and furniture were returned from Henry Harbin School, and the great day dawned at last on 27th April 1942 when the entire South Road School assembled together in their own building.

At that time it was still necessary for some of the children to use the Lagland Street school shelters during air raid warnings, but by 1st June their own shelters were ready for use, and not a day too soon for this school which had for so long been guests at Henry Harbin now had to play hosts to the juniors of St James' School. During the Blitz of Wednesday night, 3rd June, the upper floor of St James' School had been burnt out completely, and it was nine months before those children were able to occupy their own classrooms once again.

There was much re-stocking of books and equipment necessary and the sanctioned expenditure for South Road for 1942/3 was £245 in this connection. Further sums for needlework, craft, woodwork and metalwork

Staff 1946
Headmaster, Mr Hartnell with Mr Nash, Mrs Bailey, Mr Evans, Mr Brown, Mrs Fagg,
Mr Francis, Miss Harman, Miss Turner, Miss Buckmaster and Mr Beale.
Mr Francis who had just started at the school, was the son of Mr Francis who had taught at
the National, and at Henry Harbin.

were also allowed. Most of the desks which had been sent out on loan to various schools in the Borough never were returned at all. Those that were returned were either unusable or decidedly worse for wear. Replacements were needed in this direction, for numbers on the school roll now totalled 380.

Many local children had by this time been evacuated overseas as the air raids persisted. But progress was taking place and a GPO telephone was at last installed at the school. New too was the machinery being installed at the Malmesbury and Parson's Dairies, who supplied the daily milk to school children in third of a pint bottles. Unfortunately this suffered a few teething troubles', and no milk was delivered to the school for a week. When a second breakdown occurred the Headmaster suggested to the dairy that, as they were unable to deliver the milk in bottles maybe they could do so in bulk, and so for some further weeks it came to school in milk churns. Children had to bring cups to school from home to enable them to be served from the churns.

It seems that during 1942 the combination of unrest, war and the strain of the perpetual air raids, started to take its toll. Children were brought out of the shelters after an air raid warning in a half fainting condition. Benches from the school were carried into the shelters in an effort to supply some kind of seating, at least for the younger children.

It was not surprising then that attendance figures began to suffer. The Headmaster was not always satisfied that the reasons given by some of the parents were adequate. In addition, he was displeased during the mumps epidemic in the autumn, to know that any child who had been excluded from school attendance was allowed to attend the local cinemas. With his own eyes he saw children running errands or playing on the Quay when he had received a parent's note to say that the child had no boots and was therefore unable to attend school. A Medical Certificate received stating that the child had Pharyngitis (and that seems to have been the latter day equivalent of today's 'viral infection') was no safeguard against seeing the child playing out in the streets all week. Many of the children who went hop-picking at the weekends were purported not to have returned, and yet were seen from Monday onwards at home.

National events and this continued absenteeism, together with the lack of concern on the part of some of the parents to take steps to prevent the spread of epidemics, caused the Headmaster much worry. Not without cause either, for just as the mumps epidemic was beginning to subside it was learned that during the Christmas holidays of 1942 one of the pupils, Peter Clark, had died of Diphtheria.

Enemy bombs continued to drop in the near vicinity of the school, and the children were now well used to being shepherded swiftly into the shelters, whether they were in school when the Alert sounded or out in the playground. The children of St James' School were able to return to their own repaired school rooms in March, and things also brightened in the South Road shelters when in April of 1943 twelve miners' lamps replaced the hurricane lamps which had until then afforded meagre lighting during the alerts.

When Lagland Street School ran short of coal, it was from the South Road store that two loads were loaned to tide them over, and then Mr Peace and his staff went to a lot of trouble to plan yet more rearrangements to the classrooms, and worked out a fresh timetable to accommodate the 106 pupils due to be transferred from Oakdale School after the Easter break. It was not surprising that he was rather annoyed when, at the last moment, these children were switched to Courthill Junior School instead.

But the general outlook was brighter, the war for Britain was taking an upward surge, and when in May, the target for the school in a National Savings 'Wings for Victory Week' was almost trebled, the children were granted a day's holiday. Attendance also improved to the extent that at long last the school qualified once more for an Attendance half-day holiday.

January 1944 started on a happy note with the Headmaster attending his daughter's marriage. The school nurse, Nurse Lewis, left to take up her duties in London and her place was taken by Nurse Hughes, who called at the school in the accustomed manner every Friday morning. The heads of the children were examined regularly, and at one time five children were excluded on account of their verminous condition. Such children attended the school clinic to receive treatment.

But 1944 might well have been termed 'the year of the accident' at South Road School, for a procession of these took place from the mysterious fire which destroyed Mr Kay's waste paper basket and its contents badly charring a cupboard in the process, through to one day in November when a girl, Wendy Woodrow, fell when crossing the road outside school and two knitting needles she was carrying pierced her knee and bent at right angles under the flesh. Employees of Messrs Butler & Sons, who were still occupying the junction site of Green and South Roads (now school property) rushed her to Cornelia Hospital at Longfleet Road.

In between these two occurrences, Meryll Wadham (aged seven) tripped in the playground and suffered a fractured skull. Dorothy Goble was taken down the road to her mother (who was working at Poole Gas Works) after a boy had knocked a blackboard over which fell and injured her foot badly. Member of staff Mr A. G. Evans slipped and twisted his thigh in the stock room, and even Mr White the caretaker had to absent himself from duties on account of a bout of rheumatism.

The temporary assistant, when he arrived, caused the Headmaster trouble for after ten minutes' work on the furnace he advised Mr Peace that he was a storeman and not a workman. Mr Peace therefore lit all fires himself for the rest of the week, with a Mr May volunteering to help with the caretaking. Such were the trials and tribulations that at the end of that year Mr Peace himself was absent, not at all well.

Now that Flying Bombs had started to fall over London yet more refugees arrived in Poole to swell the ranks, and it became necessary to filter the special Class IIIC pupils into the IIIB and IVB classes.

The classes, with their teachers, were then as follows :

IVA	=	Miss Turner
IVB	=	Mrs Dominey
IIIA	=	Miss Buckmaster
IIIB	=	Mr Beale
IIA	=	Mr Evans
IIB	=	Miss Arnold
IA	=	Mrs Fagg
IB	=	Mr Kay

More desks and a portable wireless set were acquired and in early 1945 work commenced on the building of an extension for washing-up etc. in preparation for the provision of school mid-day meals.

In February, the Sea Cadets Corps, who had been using the school temporarily for their meetings, moved all their belongings to the adjacent Drill Hall, and summer hours were once again worked at the school, i.e. 9 a.m. – 12 noon and 1.45 p.m. – 4 p.m.

Great rejoicing – VE Day on 8th May 1945! As the following day was Ascension Day, two days' holiday were enjoyed.

And then in June the 'Meals in Schools' scheme started on the premises

1948, Mr. Beale (L), and Mr. Hartnell (R), with mixed class of juniors.
Names recalled: T. Archer, K. Swan, G. Tilsed, Brett, T. Roper, G. Clapp,
Emerson twins, D. Bailey.

with 191 out of the 329 pupils availing themselves of the facility. Tickets sold in school were exchanged for the main course (1/1 ld) and the pudding (5d). On the first day of the scheme, the meal started to be served at 12.15 p.m. but on account of a shortage of plates, which had to be washed–up hastily and re-used as the meal progressed, the children were not out of the Dining Room until 1.25 p.m. By the time the teaching staff had eaten it was well after 2 p.m. when school recommenced that day. When Mr Bond, the Catering Manager, visited later in the afternoon he agreed that more plates were required and that the Hot Plate would give more service in the Dining Room instead of the kitchen annexe.

Before the end of 1945 Miss K. Arnold, Mr McG. Kay and Mr Peace had all resigned, Mr Beale gave up his duties as Acting Deputy Headmaster, and on 5th November Mr C. L. Hartnell took over the Headship.

One of his first innovations was to alter the starting time to 9.25 a.m. to bring South Road School into line with the other schools in the vicinity.

The swimming lessons, which had until now been Mr Hartnell's responsibility, were now in charge of Mr Beale as they were held on Mondays, Tuesdays and Thursdays in the afternoon and so took up quite a slice of teaching time.

In 1946, Peace was celebrated on Victory Day, 8th June. The Annual Country Dance Festival at Bovington became a Victory occasion. The Country Dance routine was performed at a Garden Party and the proceeds donated to the Cornelia Hospital. The Authorities lost no time in taking steps to demolish the school shelters, and at times the din was disruptive to school study. During the period when the Headmaster was attending a Ministry of Education course at Chichester, Mrs Hartnell helped out as a Supply Teacher in Class IIIB. Mr Francis commenced duties in September (and continued at the school until his retirement in September 1980). In order to keep the children well occupied and off the streets during the winter months, evening classes were started quite voluntarily by some of the staff. For example, Miss Buckmaster took 30 girls in Needlework and Weaving each Monday evening. Mr Evans helped a lucky 25 boys in Handicrafts ('lucky' because 120 boys and girls applied to attend) – and Mrs Dominey and Mrs Fagg took a class in Country Dancing. These classes were popular and well attended right up to the Christmas break when all the classes enjoyed their customary parties.

Despite all the strides made in the Education world, including the raising of school leaving age to 15, in January 1947 a boy called Edward Baker aged 11 years 2 months started at South Road School having never attended school before! It reflected credit on the Staff and pupils that he settled in so well.

Mr Keith A. P. Smith (Son of H. P. Smith) commenced duties as a temporary teacher in Class IIA in March 1947, and the post of School Secretary held by Miss June Tilsed since 1946 was filled by Miss Pamela Cull, an ex-pupil of Henry Harbin Girls' School. During the summer term three students from Salisbury Training College (the Misses Truss, Williams and Swain) spent three weeks' teaching practice at the school. Erection of a new purpose built Dining Hall was commenced, and when Mr David Hall, a reporter from a New York newspaper, visited for a day early in July he showed great interest in these plans, and indeed of the school in general, with a special emphasis being placed on the Handicrafts.

At the beginning of the Autumn term of 1947, two new female teachers started, Miss D. M. Dacombe and Miss M. Phillips, from the now closed St James' School.

The Staff of South Road School in September 1947 was as follows :
Headmaster C. L. Hartnell

IVA	=	Miss R. Turner – 40 on the roll
IVB	=	Mrs E. Dominey – 40 on the roll
IIIA	=	Miss E. Buckmaster – 39 on the roll
IIIB	=	Mr B. Bale – 40 on the roll
IIIC	=	Mr W. Andrews – 37 on the roll
IIA	=	Miss B. Harman – 42 on the roll
IIB	=	Mr L. Brown – 41 on the roll
IIC	=	Mr H. Francis – 30 on the roll
IA	=	Mrs G. Fagg – 37 on the roll
IB	=	Mrs D. Bailey – 41 on the roll
IC	=	Miss D. Dacombe – 38 on the roll

ID   =   Miss M. Phillips – 32 on the roll

Temporary Teachers Mr D. Nash and Mr K. Smith

Handicrafts Mr Evans

Of these 457 pupils, 300 stayed to school dinner and because the new Dining Hall was not then finished they had to be accommodated in the downstair classrooms and corridors. It was not occupied until October when it was opened in a flurry of officialdom including the Mayor, the Borough Education Officer (Mr Higham), the Secretary of the Local National Savings Committee (Mr Bodiley), and the Correspondent of the School Managers (Mr A. F. Roberts) attending. This proved an excellent opportunity to address the pupils on the necessity to save, and was the start of a week's 'Save for the Silver Lining' campaign.

Her Royal Highness the Princess Elizabeth married Lieutenant Philip Mountbatten on 20th November of this year, when a day's holiday was granted to enable the children to participate in the various festivities arranged in this area.

Food and clothes were still rationed but there was a concession for children who grew too quickly to apply for supplementary clothing coupons, and these were issued from the schools on Form O C/4 D.

Although the Dining Hall was not to be completely finished until late 1948, everyone was delighted after the Christmas break to find that a bit of warmth in the form of gas heaters had by then been installed.

Corporal punishment was still meted out on occasions and 'swearing in the playground' was one of the offences. Thanks to the enthusiasm of Mr Hartnell, South Road was the first Junior School to possess a Ciné Projector, and this was put to good use during the winter evenings at school when films were shown to the children on Friday nights for the sum of about twopence. Most of the films shown were loaned by various organisations and by Kodak. This Cinematograph was also taken on occasions to the neighbouring schools by Mr Hartnell.

South Road sent a choir of 40 to the Schools' Musical Festival held at the Great Hall of Parkstone Grammar School, and two teams were taken by Miss Turner and Miss Buckmaster to the County Drama Festival at Dorchester. The school celebrated the Royal Silver Wedding of King George VI and Queen Elizabeth in April by outdoor Country Dancing to music supplied by the school gramophone and amplifier. But in June everyone was saddened at the death of the late Headmaster, Mr Peace, and Staff and pupils sent a wreath.

By September, the 70 or so children who had been attending from Oakdale School for the past year returned to that school, and the numbers at South Road dropped once more to 357. This was short lived however, for in November, accompanied by teachers, Mrs Short and Miss Matthews, two classes from the St Peter's Voluntary Primary School shared the South Road premises whilst theirs were undergoing repairs and redecoration. These children (again about 70) although remaining on St Peter's register, were filtered into six first and second year classes.

During the Christmas holiday of 1948 the ground floor premises of South Road were redecorated, but the Headmaster's pleasure was soon to be blighted for he discovered, a week after school recommenced in January 1949, that his room had been broken into by way of the window. The School Post Office Savings Book, a box of drawing instruments and several keys were missing.

An epidemic of mumps was prevalent, and poor Mr Hartnell, the Headmaster, succumbed in March. And then in April the St Peter's children returned to their own school, leaving South Road to carry on intact once again. At the County Sports in June, Diana Davis won the girls high jump at 4 feet, and Creigton Cross was third in the boys' high jump at 3 feet 11 inches. Throughout July children from the various classes visited Badbury Rings, London Zoo, Corfe Castle, and the Pitt-Rivers Museum. Several children displayed weaving, spinning and needlework at a Handicraft Exhibition in the Poole Park, and on the 21st July the Schools' Swimming Championship was won by Peter Smith.

As 1950 unfolded spirits were high and pupils and staff alike had little cause to complain at the conditions existing at school. So many cups and trophies had been won by the children for South Road that it became necessary to get an insurance company representative to call and assess their value. Even the backward children were now being given special teaching attention, and any child with a speech defect was attended to by two ladies from the Speech Therapy Clinic. Now that the school had the South Road premises to itself, there was adequate room for teaching as well as Physical Education, music, and arts and crafts, plus other extra mural activities.

The children who took part in the special Remedial Exercise class thoroughly enjoyed the participation, and rejoiced when their specially trained teacher, Miss Dacombe, was married during the Easter vacation of 1950 and returned to school as Mrs D Christopher.

The Staff rooms, cloak rooms, dining room and lavatory amenities were far superior to most of the other schools in the Borough at that time. The lighting (soon to be switched to fluorescent lighting), and the heating were adequate, and the playground was of sufficient size to allow ball games and sports training to take place. The annual school outing to a place of interest continued to be enjoyed, as were the Country Folk Dance Festival and the Christmas Concert. Parents seemed to become more and more interested in the school's activities, and Open Days were always well attended. Even the school outings became popular with some parents who accompanied their offspring in the summer of 1950 to Windsor. They all journeyed by train from Poole, and had a conducted tour of the Castle followed by tea on a river steamer going down the Thames to Runnymede.

It was on this happy note that Miss E M Buckmaster, who had spent 52 years teaching in Poole at South Road and the old British School before it, retired. She was presented with an electric tea-making and alarm set by the

Chairman of the Managers, Alderman Joe Bright (of Bright's Bread and Cake Shop in High Street below the Post Office).

The number of pupils on the roll at the end of 1950 was 346, and it had been decided to renumber the classes from 1 to 11, Class 1 being at the top end in the place of the old IVA. The teachers were arranged as follows :

Class 1	Miss R. Turner	36
Class 2	Miss E. Dominey	35
Class 3	Mr B. Bale	33
Class 4	Mr L. Roche	30
Class 5	Mr W. Marshall	27
Class 6	Mr A. Evans	38
Class 7	Mr L. Brown	33
Class 8	Mr H. Francis	25
Class 9	Mrs G. Fagg	33
Class 10	Mrs D. Bailey	32
Class 11	Miss K. Barrington	24

with the addition of Mrs Christopher who took music and the Remedial Classes together with certain oral lessons.

The Remedial Class children acted as a Demonstration Class to a lecture given at the Lagland Street School in February 1951.

During June, Mr Francis had to be away on National Service 'Z' reserve call-up scheme, and Miss Turner and Miss Barrington took 42 children to the Dorset County School site at Carey Camp near Wareham for a week. Also during June, 40 children with 3 teachers visited the *'Festival of Britain'* Pleasure Gardens at Battersea, London, and visited the South Bank *'Festival of Britain'* Exhibition.

Just before Christmas tins of beefsteak received from Australia as a gift, were distributed amongst the children. Also about this time two Heads of Technical Institutes from Berlin visited the school to observe English methods of teaching.

By the start of 1952 there were 383 children on the register, and most were present to pay respect to the memory of King George VI on 6th February. After a short service all stood in silence for a few moments. The reign of Queen Elizabeth II had now begun.

The kaleidoscope of school life continued. Miss Anita Franklin, the clerical assistant, resigned and her place was taken by Mrs Hilda Blackmore. Mr Beale, who was taken ill at the end of 1952, died on the morning of 8th January 1953, aged 54.

1953 was Coronation Year, but before school broke up on 22nd May for the Whitsun break and Coronation holidays the school mourned the loss of one of its most illustrious Headmasters, Mr H. P. Smith; MBE, JP, BA, FCP, who died in April. Everyone knew that he was a very sick man when he

Staff 1959 September
Back row: Mr. Francis, Mrs. Fagg, Mr. Brown, Mr. Haines, Mr. Withey. Centre row:
Miss Barrington, Mrs. McCallum, Mrs. Bartlett, Mrs. Blackmore, Miss Foxall,
Mrs. Orfield. Front row: Mrs. Bailey, Mrs Munden, Mr. Marshall, Mr. Hartnell (Head).
Mr. Evans, Miss Memory, Mrs. Barrett, with the caretaker, Mr. Mitchell.

attended the *'Pageant of Poole'* the previous year in the Poole Park. He had written the script for the nine episodes. It was indeed fortunate that a man who had done so much for Poole should have lived to see its history re-enacted in Pageant form on the green slopes by the edge of the Park Lake that he loved and indeed had lived beside. Miss Gwen Lalley had directed the Pageant in which many of the inhabitants of Poole took part, and when the colour film of it was ready it was shown to all the schools. Later in the year, the children of South Road took part in their own Pageant entitled *'Children of History'*. About 500 parents and friends watched as the children mimed their parts to a previously recorded tape. As this was held in June and the weather was good, it took place in the playground.

The evening before, about 100 pupils had attended a mass Coronation Display of school children at Poole Stadium. Later in the month a holiday was granted to enable anyone to attend the Coronation Naval Review at Spithead. It was not until 3rd July that the Chairman of the School Managers, Alderman J. Bright, JP, managed to get to South Road to distribute Coronation Mugs. About a week later, a monochrome version of the Coronation Ceremony Film was shown to the Lagland Street and South Road scholars in the school dining hall.

During all these activities Mrs Christopher resigned to give birth, and her place was taken by Mrs Beryl J. Allen of Salterns Road, Parkstone.

There were still eleven classes for the 389 children. Miss Turner was Deputy Head and Mr A. G. Evans was First Assistant. The year ended happily, with all the children attending the Mario Puppet Show in Bournemouth, and then holding a Carol Service in the Hall on the last day of term.

With numbers on the roll reaching 394, Mr Hartnell decided at the beginning of 1954 to have 12 classes in future. Nearly all of the children went to the Regent Cinema at the top end of High Street (now the site of Boots in the Dolphin Centre), during February to watch the film *"The Conquest of Everest"*, news of which had come through on Coronation Day the previous year.

The weather was cold and the playground covered in patches of ice. The outside toilets had frozen and this kept the caretaker busy with buckets of water carried out to flush them. It seems unfortunate that later in the year, after complaints about the state of the lavatories, he, together with two women cleaners, sent in a week's notice. Then a temporary caretaker, Mr N Taylor from Henry Harbin School, helped out until another temporary help came from the Poole Grammar School in the form of Mr Mitchell aided by two new lady cleaners, Mrs Gleed and Mrs Pike.

Road Safety had by now become a favourite topic for talks, and the police frequently checked bicycles that children had ridden to school to ensure that they were in a safe and road-worthy condition. After giving the pupils one such lecture on road safety, a Mr O. Ellum was taken ill as he left school and everyone was distressed to learn of his death the next day.

Another death which was mourned by staff and scholars alike was that of Mr A. J. Martin who had been Headmaster of the school from 1939 to 1942, and before that at the "National". Mr Hartnell and two members of the staff attended his funeral on 27th October 1954.

Poole in this year had its first Labour Mayor, Alderman Fred Reeves, MM, (his daughter Margaret had attended the school earlier) and he together with his wife made the Prize Presentations throughout their term of office.

Just before Christmas, the old grand piano now unplayable, but which had seen a deal of life and had been lovingly tuned every Spring, was sent across to Herbert Carter School for use as scrap material.

During 1955 Miss K. Barrington took part in an exchange-teaching scheme in Ontario, Canada, and her place at South Road for the year was taken by Miss Irene Plantz.

The optional evening classes (which had been started during the winter of 1946) were again well supported. So much so that it became necessary to start an additional needlework class to accommodate all those wishing to attend. Much of their work was shown at County exhibitions. The girls enjoying the more sporting activities were also bringing honours to the

Netball Team 1955/56
Back row: Mrs. Lees, Maureen Salter, Dianne Cooper with County Shield, Jackie Edwards.
Front row: Val Coles, Marion Biles with League Cup, Pat Vincent, Carol Miles with
Knockout Cup, Pat Culter. First school to win all three in one year.

school. In 1955 the Netball Team were the first to win the County Shield, the League Cup and the Knockout Cup all in one year. Each member was presented with a gold medal by the Mayor in his Parlour. Boxing had become a favourite sport with the schools, and South Road boys were in the forefront of the contenders. Boys taking part in the Tournaments were always inspected by the Medical Officer a few hours before they were due to fight to ensure they were fit to participate. Early in 1956 Mr Francis escorted boy boxers from the Poole schools to Newquay to take part in the South West Regional Championships. The Football scene too, had widened its horizons, for Mr Marshall went with the Poole Schools' Football Team when they played Liverpool schools at Liverpool. The keen ones were also spectators, for on 26th April some 20 boys together with 2 masters attended the England v. Scotland Schoolboy International game in London.

Miss Plantz, the exchange teacher, was granted leave of absence during the last days of June to travel up to London to attend a gathering at Lambeth Palace. There she was presented to the Queen Mother, and later, on 19th July, she attended a Garden Party at Buckingham Palace. This was a great finale to her year in England, and when school started again in September after the summer recess, Miss Barrington was once again back at South Road. New teachers, Mrs Oldfield and Mrs Barrett started at the same time, and Mr W. Marshall had been chosen by Mr Hartnell to act as his Deputy Head in the place of Miss Turner who, after 39 years at the school, had retired. She had been presented with a fireside armchair and an occasional table by the Mayor, Councillor C. W. Wells, during the Prize Distributions at the end of term. Mrs Lee too had left the staff, expecting a baby, and she and Miss Plantz were given ornamental vases of Branksome Pottery.

And so in September 1956 the 379 pupils had quite a new look staff. But the routine was familiar, with the School Dentist and Medical Officer calling periodically. The Christmas service this year held in the Methodist Church, High Street, raised £6. 4. 4d. for the Royal National Institute for the Blind, and after the Christmas party each child received ice cream and a box of chocolates.

Another new face to appear on the scene early in 1957 was a boy aged nine years, a Hungarian refugee, who could speak no English. Two additional teachers were taken on in September, Mr Withey and Mrs Tasker. Mrs Tasker's stay was very short-lived for she was transferred within a week to Broadstone County Primary School, and her place taken by Mrs Munden. The classes had once again been re-arranged and now the staffing was as follows:

4A	=	Mrs Dominey
4B	=	Mrs Oldfield
4C	=	Mr Brown
3A	=	Mr Evans
3B	=	Miss Barrington
3C	=	Mr Withey
2A	=	Mr Roche
2B	=	Mrs Barrett
2C	=	Mr Francis
2D	=	Miss Derbyshire
1A	=	Mrs Fagg
1B	=	Mrs Bailey
1C	=	Mrs Tasker

Romance had bloomed between members of staff, Mr Francis and Miss Derbyshire, who were married during the Christmas break. Miss Derbyshire was transferred to the Martin Road School, and so when school recommenced in January 1958 yet another teacher, Mrs G. M. Bartlett, joined the staff. But in July Mrs Dominey retired, having been on the staff for twenty years. She was presented with a bookcase and an easy chair. Mr Roche was given a wrist watch on his departure to take up his new appointment as Deputy Head of St Peter's School, Parkstone.

School premises were once again stretched at the seams at the beginning of the autumn term 1958, for a large number of children were for a time sent to South Road from Waterloo Estate. The numbers reached 520 and it was necessary to house Classes 2B, 2C and 2D in the three rooms at the Lagland Street School. The staff were now :- Mrs Oldfield, Miss Barrington, Mr Brown, Mr Evans, Mrs Snowdon, Mr Withey, Mrs Fagg, Mr Haines, Mr Francis, Mrs Bartlett, Mrs Sayer, Miss Memory, Mrs Bailey, Mrs Munden, and Mrs McCallum.

Separate staff were now employed under "Circular 97" to attend the playground and supervise the children at lunchtime. Mrs E. Slade and Mrs S. Allen undertook these duties in October.

In November, a deputation from Dorset County Education Committee inspected the school with a view to rehabilitation. In the party were Mr J. Collins, Mr J. B. Chesterfield, Mr F. C. Day, Sir Theodore Tasker, Mr T. L. Higham, Councillor Miss Jeanne Bisgood JP, and Mr Robert Hawker (Deputy Borough Engineer).

For a short time at the beginning of 1959 Miss Turner, who had taught so diligently at the school and had retired in 1956, worked as relief clerical assistant in the absence of Mrs Blackmore who had been taken ill and was obliged to spend some time in hospital. Yellow House, now re-named St David's, once again won the School Sports Championship.

By the autumn term when Miss Jean Foxhall had replaced Mrs Snowdon, and there were 483 children on the books, the staff were:

Head C.L. Hartnell;

Deputy W.Marshall

1a	=	Mrs J.A. Barrett
1b	=	Miss J. Foxhall
1c	=	Mrs D.C. Bailey
1d	=	Mrs D F. Munden
1e	=	Mrs D.M. McCallum
2a	=	Mrs G. N. Fagg
2b	=	Mr B.B. Haines
2c	=	Mr H.R.B. Francis
2d	=	Mrs G.M. Bartlett
3a	=	Mrs K.D. Oldfield
3b	=	Miss J. Memory
3c	=	Mr H. N. Withey
4a	=	Miss K. Barrington
4b	=	Mr A. G. Evans
4c	=	Mr L. J. Brown

The evening play centre classes continued successfully from Monday to Thursday covering crafts, needlework, music and PE. An old pupil, Mr W.S.

Rockett who, during the early 1930's, had carried off so many swimming honours, visited school in October to give a talk to the third and fourth year pupils. He had swum the English Channel in 1950 and was at the time official coach for aspiring cross-channel swimmers.

During 1959 the newly appointed Education Officer was Mr Arthur. A. Ingham. At the end of the year the 3a teacher, Mrs Oldfield, was presented with a Poole pottery vase when she left. Her place was taken by Mrs D.A. Roche at commencement of school in 1960, but unfortunately she had to have major surgery in March and a Mr Williams came as her supply replacement.

When school broke up for Easter holidays, Mrs Bailey retired having taught for fifteen years, but she was soon to be back again acting as a supply. Mrs McCallum got a teaching post at Upton, and she also left. This vacancy was filled by Miss O. Mackel.

During June a general Inspection of school was carried out by Miss Berwick, Mr Todd and Mr Busby, and in July Coco, the famous clown, came to talk to the children on Road Safety. Next day, 200 of the children went along to the Bertram Mills Circus to see him perform. Not long afterwards, Mr B. Haines was taken ill and was absent, off and on, for the best part of a year, by which time Miss Jean Memory had become Mrs Willis and Miss D. Spencer had joined the staff.

A new wing of Poole Hospital was opened in May of 1961. Two hundred South Road children lined the route taken by HRH Princess Alexandra, who performed the Opening Ceremony. The school annual outing that year was to the London Zoo, 350 children and parents participated.

During this year extensive alterations were made to the South Road buildings. These included new inside toilets for both the boys and girls, a new staff room, office, and a storeroom. All this had taken some weeks, and when the work was almost complete at the beginning of July, intruders gained access through a temporary opening, plugged a sink, then turned the taps on full. As a consequence when the caretaker arrived next morning, he found the ground floor corridor and several classrooms flooded. It took until eleven o'clock to mop and clean up.

Diphtheria injections and anti-polio vaccines were administered during the summer months to the majority of the pupils. Mr Haines continued to suffer very poor health and his death was mourned in October by staff and children alike. The number on the roll had now fallen to 394 as no first year children were coming in from Waterloo Estate. The new Hillbourne Junior School received two of the South Road staff, Mrs J. Barrett and Miss O. Mackel. Miss J. Foxhall left to emigrate to Australia.

By the summer term of 1962 the numbers at South Road had dwindled to 234, for when the new Junior School opened at Hillbourne, Waterloo, 151 children had been transferred. The staff remaining at South Road was then as follows:

4a	=	Mr Marshall
4b	=	Mr Evans
4c	=	Mr Brown
4d	=	Mr Francis
Class 3	=	Mrs Roche
Class 2	=	Mrs Fagg
Class 1	=	Mrs Bartlett

Mrs Christopher attended on Tuesday and Wednesday mornings to teach music. It was during this term that preliminary discussions took place regarding the possible merging of South Road and Lagland Street Infants' School. This was indeed implemented after the summer vacation when the school changed its format and became South Road Mixed Junior and Infants' School.

South Road Mixed Junior and Infants' School

When school reopened on 6th September 1962 the infants from Lagland Street Infants' School had been amalgamated into the South Road School. There were 152 juniors and 64 infants divided into 5 junior classes and 2 infants' classes, with teaching staff as follows :

Class 4a	=	Mrs Roche
Class 4b	=	Mr H.R.B. Francis
Class 3	=	Mr W. Marshall
Class 2	=	Mr A.G. Evans
Class 1	=	Mrs G.N. Fagg
6th(Infants)	=	Miss D. White
7th(Infants)	=	Miss S. Lamb

Mrs G. Bartlett had retired at the end of July, as had the school caretaker, Mr G.W. Mitchell. Mr J. Aldous acted as a temporary school caretaker until the appointment of a Mr J. Painton in November.

100 children from the St. Mary's Roman Catholic School joined South Road Juniors in appreciating a concert by the String Quartet of the Bournemouth Symphony Orchestra which was given just before Christmas 1962.

When the new term started in 1963 another class had been formed in the Infants' Department to accommodate children coming in from Turlin Moor at Hamworthy. Mrs Rogers started as a supply teacher, which was just as well for the number of infants jumped to 115. A speech therapist paid regular visits to children suspected of having less than normal hearing. They were given audiogram tests by Mrs Real, or the aptly named Miss Tone.

At last the outdoor toilets, which had been falling rapidly into a state of disrepair and had become a health hazard, were demolished.

In view of the large percentage of children now in possession of a bicycle, and the greatly increased road traffic, the police started cycle training classes. After a course of six evenings of instruction, the police tested the children and awarded marks out of 100. Those with a sufficiently high pass mark were awarded badges and certificates. Coco, the Clown from Bertram Mills Circus, played his part again by coming along during school hours to talk to the children.

National Savings' Stamps and Certificates were still sold at school each week, and there was keen competition between the local schools to reach good targets. South Road was particularly pleased when, early in 1964, two Regional Commissioners from the National Savings' Movement came along to present the Sheriff Cole Cup to the school.

After Easter 1964 the number of infants jumped ahead of the juniors, with 169 as opposed to 143. Mr Evans, member of staff since 1927 retired and was presented with a wrist watch and travelling case.

Mr Hartnell, the Headmaster, was presented with many gifts from Managers, parents, staff and children on his retirement at break-up of school in July 1964. Albert Thomas Goodman took over as Headmaster from 8th September 1964, with Miss R. A. Power as assistant. Another part-time assistant, Mrs S. M. Hollingsworth started, to join Mrs D. M. Christopher whose teaching sessions increased from two to three.

The staffing situation was then as follows:

INFANTS

Class 9	=	Miss S. E. Lamb	34 on the Roll
Class 8	=	Miss R. A. Power	36 on the Roll
Class 7	=	Miss D. White	38 on the Roll
(In charge of Infants)			
Class 6	=	Mrs P. Rogers	34 on the Roll
Class 5	=	Mrs J. Saunders	32 on the Roll

JUNIORS

Class 1	=	Mrs G. N. Fagg	39 on the Roll
Class 2	=	Mr H. R. B. Francis	37 on the Roll
Class 3	=	Mrs D. A. Roche	39 on the Roll
Class 4	=	Mr W. Marshall	30 on the Roll

Part Time Teachers - Mrs D. M. Christopher,
Mrs S. M. Hollingsworth
School Caretaker - Mr J. Painton
School Secretary - Mrs H. Blackmore.

It was during this period that the school colours were changed from old gold/black to blue.

Soon after school re-opened, the repairs and maintenance surveyor, Mr Maurice Scollick, the Youth Officer Mr Ken Whiteside together with the Headmaster, inspected the Drill Hall with a view to suggesting alterations necessary to bring it in to use as a school hall and youth centre.

The General Election of 15th October meant that school closed all day, but a few days later telephone engineers called to extend the school's telephone system and update the equipment. The school was due for a facelift inside and out and towards the end of 1964 the broken fence around the playground was repaired. The sink and gas point from the old walk-in cupboard on the upper floor was removed and decorating began in Classroom

Netball Team 1963
Captain Linda Foster hold cup.

3. Mrs Roche and pupils had vacated this room and moved down to the Lagland Street premises.

Classroom 3, when redecorated, was successively used by all the other classes in turn as their own rooms were being decorated during term time. When school broke up for the Christmas recess, Mrs D. A. Roche left and she was replaced by Mr W. T. Williams in the new year, 1965. Another Infants' Class was set up at Lagland Street with Mrs G. M. Packman as its teacher. During the Christmas break the workmen had been busy and every classroom had been fitted with a display board. The open fireplace in the Headmaster's room was removed, the room was rewired and a nine-foot high fake ceiling was put in.

Numbers were still on the increase and stood at 350 on the Roll. To assist with the greatly increased number of children staying to school dinner, a further dining room assistant was hired.

Early in the year the Initial Teaching Alphabet (ITA) was introduced into the Infants' Class 9. This was Miss Lamb's Class which now accommodated all the South Road non-readers. All the Turlin Moor non-readers were put together in a newly formed Class 10.

Regular visitors to the school now included the Educational Psychologist, Mr J. Foster, who carried out ascertainment tests on all retarded pupils, and the Audio-Therapist, Mrs Real, who tested the hearing ability of the children.

The school was saddened and shocked to hear of the tragedy that befell two of its pupils on Saturday, 12th June 1965. One of the school prefects, Pat Mowlam, and Martin Liddell, recently transferred to South Road from Hamworthy, were both burned to death in a terrible fire at the Old Town Cafe at the bottom of High Street, together with a third child. When the funeral took place on the 16th at St. James' Church, the Headmaster, five staff and five children from the top class attended. The other big fire which affected South Road was that which had gutted the adjacent Butler's Brush Factory. Part of the site was later taken over by the school.

Rain fell heavily during July, the Infants' Sports were cancelled and the campers who had set off for Carey had a very dampened week. A sixth form student from the Henry Harbin School, Miss Valerie Harrex, spent a week's observation at South Road school prior to entering her Teacher Training Course at St. Gabriel's College, London. This had become common practice with student teachers destined for various colleges.

By the autumn term of 1965, the numbers had swollen to 436. Yet another new Infants' Class was formed making the number up to seven, with the same five Junior classes. The teacher for the new class was Miss E. J. Penter. In view of the overcrowding at the South Road premises, three of the Infants' classes were held at the Lagland Street School premises. The Remedial Group were taught by Mrs S. M. Hollingsworth in the converted staff room on the upper floor.

During 16th, 17th and 18th November a full inspection of school took place. HM Inspectors, Miss Berwick, Mr Davies, and Mr Hilton officiated. During this time the children who were eligible sat their Second Verbal Reasoning Test for the 11 plus examination. They had taken the first part in late October.

Christmas celebrations were held at both Lagland Street and South Road. The Juniors presented their Christmas Festival of Carols and Nativity Play at the Skinner Street Congregational Church.

On 21st December when school broke up for Christmas, Miss D. M. White retired after forty years' teaching, first at Lagland Street and latterly at South Road. Miss Jeanne Bisgood, Chairman of the Education Committee, visited to bid farewell and presentations were made on behalf of the children, staff, and the Managers.

In January 1966, with the numbers standing at 437, two more teachers Miss A.H.M. Ash and Miss P. Vasidis started. This month also saw the formation of a Parent-Teachers Association (PTA). Mr Coulson, a parent, was elected as Chairman and a group formed themselves into an Executive Committee to arrange a programme of activities (some fund-raising) to take place over the year.

In March 153 infants left on transfer to the recently completed Turlin Moor Primary School at Hamworthy. Four teachers, Mrs G. J. Packman, Mrs E. Simmons, Miss E. J. Penter and Miss Vasidis transferred with them.

When school resumed in April after the Easter break, it was the turn of children from yet another new Estate to share the South Road premises. This term a unit of Canford Heath children was set up under a new member of staff, Mrs G. F. Joy.

All the pupils were well entertained during the first half of the year. They received a magician, Richard Barr, who cleverly built an entertainment around the Highway Code. The Wessex String Quartet gave a concert for the scholars in June, as did the Theatre for Youth Company who performed *"Magic Circle"*. Class 7 paid a visit to Oakdale Creameries one morning, and 250 children and parents toured the Isle of Wight on 15th July. The PTA. contribution was a river trip to Wareham one evening in June.

When school broke up for the summer holidays Miss S.E. Lamb, Miss R.A. Power and Mrs P. Rogers left to take up appointments in other schools. At the Leavers' Service, attended by the Mayor and Mayoress, one of the pupils, Susan Loving, was presented with the Gold Award of the Amateur Swimming Association. This was the first time this award had been presented to a Primary School child in Poole. This event was however repeated in 1968 when Pauline Oliver was awarded the Gold Award.

The Canford Heath contingent continued to swell the South Road ranks, and for the autumn term an additional class under Mrs Sidoli was formed to accommodate them. A separate class for sub-normal children was set up in the charge of Mrs G.N. Fagg. Four other new members of staff were Miss A.E. Haysom (Head of Infants' Dept.), Miss A.J. Punter, Miss P.M. Brixey and Miss C.B. Hicks.

It was during this term that discussion of the Borough Working Party Report on Secondary Education began regarding re-organisation of secondary education in Poole. At an evening PTA meeting in September the majority of parents voted in favour of developing a form of comprehensive education based on Comprehensive Schools with an age range of 11 - 16 years, and a separate 6th form college. The alternative, to develop along the present selective system, attracted only 2 votes.

Later in September a chickenpox epidemic swept through the school, but it had passed by the time HRH Princess Margaret officially opened the new Poole Grammar School, on 11th October, at Gravel Hill. That same afternoon the pupils of South Road were out in force to help line the approach road to the new Nurses' Home which the Princess visited.

Now that the alterations to the Drill Hall adjacent to the school had been completed, it was able to be put to use as a Play Centre Club.

The Parent-Teacher Association was very active at this time both in its interest in the school activities, and also on the social side. They held *"Any Questions"* evenings with such guest speakers as the Educational Psychologist, Heads of neighbouring schools, civic dignitaries, and newswriters present. They held lively debates on such subjects as the Initial Teaching Alphabet – and any social activity they held produced a profit which was handed over to the school funds. Fashion Shows and Wine and Cheese parties were also on

1962/63 Boys' Football Team with League Champion Cup.

the agenda.

The Cosmic Crayon Company organised an Art Workshop for interested teachers in the Borough. This was held during two evenings at South Road, and was run jointly by the Head and Mr Murray of Hamworthy School. This was a very successful venture, and at a later date similar events were planned both by the Cosmic Crayon Company and by George Rowney Ltd.

At commencement of the year 1967 the numbers on the roll stood at 284. Three new staff, Mr A.R. Brook, Mrs S. Humfries and Mrs J.D. Ball started and a new class was established for Canford Heath children at Lagland Street. These children joined the main body of South Road at a concert given in the School Hall by a Brass Ensemble of the Bournemouth Symphony Orchestra on the morning of 26th May. The same day school closed for the new Spring Half Term holiday, which replaced the old Whitsun break.

St George's House won the Sports Shield this summer, and the school was placed third in the Town Primary School Sports in June.

Visits were arranged by the various classes to Southampton for a conducted tour of the cruise liner *Iberia,* to Shell Bay and the Old Town, to Wimborne Minster (where the Infants visited the Model Village) and Badbury Rings. Juniors were taken to Heathrow Airport and Windsor to enjoy a trip by steamer down the Thames. And so to the summer holidays of 1967.

On resumption of schooling for the autumn term, staff and pupils were arranged as before the break, but disruption came early in term when the

National Union of Teachers (NUT) withdrew all its Poole Members from participating in the school meals service. As a consequence, with no-one to supervise the children during lunch break, the local Education Authority decided to suspend the school meals service at several local schools including South Road. At lunch time all the children were escorted to the gates and seen off the premises. The gates were then locked until ten minutes before resumption of afternoon school. At the Lagland Street annexe, the school bus ran its return service at the end of the morning school instead of the customary 3.45 p.m.. As it was then up to the parents of these children to arrange for the return to and collection from afternoon classes, it was not surprising that only ten of the 93 children were present for the afternoon sessions. After two days it was decided to re-arrange the school sessions for Infants and for Juniors to enable them to stagger their lunch breaks. By this means teachers were continuously on the premises during school hours. This arrangement continued until early December when the dispute was resolved, and normal school and meal times were able to be resumed.

When school broke-up for Christmas Mrs Hilda Blackmore, after fourteen years' service as School Secretary, retired. She was presented with a transistor radio by Mr W.S. Rigler, Chairman of the School Managers. One of the staff, Mrs S.R. Humfries transferred to Alderney School. Her place was taken in 1968 by Mrs S. Edwards, and the new part-time Secretary was Mrs J. Parker.

A problem at the start of 1968 was the increased traffic flow up Lagland Street due to the recent introduction of one-way traffic in the Town Centre. To safeguard the children crossing this busy road, the Road Safety Officer agreed that a Road Crossing Patrol should be employed near the Foundry Arms. A Mr L. Williams commenced these duties in May.

When the summer term commenced a member of staff, Mr A.R. Brook, had taken up his new post as Deputy Head of St Joseph's School, Parkstone.

There were 260 children in the main school and 110 at the Lagland Street annexe. A Pre-School Play Group for the Canford Heath Infants was held at the St George's Hall, Oakdale, and the Headmaster together with Miss Haysom visited and kept them advised as to future policies.

During this term, the teaching of French was introduced into the curriculum of Primary Schools. Two new members joined the staff in September, Mr P. Hough and Miss J.M. Le Sueur. Numbers now stood at 385 and there were twelve classes in all. The main South Road school accommodated eight classes, including the special class for ESN children and four classes in the Lagland Street annexe. New blocks of flats erected near the schools were by now being occupied and it was felt necessary to safeguard the tenants by erecting a tall chain-link fence around both school playgrounds.

With a view to introducing Family Service at the lunch time meal in place of the Cafeteria system now in use, an additional hot plate was installed in the school kitchen. With funds provided by the PTA, book shelves and work tops in the upper corridor were installed for use by the youngest juniors.

As the Headmaster was successful in his application for the post of Head at Hayling County Primary School, Hampshire, he relinquished his Headship of South Road School on 31st December 1968, and when school recommenced on 7th January 1969 it was Mr W. Marshall who was acting Headmaster until Mr Ronald Frank Adlem was able to take up the Headship on 22nd April 1969. Mr Marshall then took over as acting Headmaster of the newly formed Canford Heath Primary School housed at the Lagland Street premises, until the new Head, Mr A.W. Ballard, commenced his appointment on 9th September 1969 at the new Canford Heath School. Mr Marshall was assisted by Mr Francis and both returned to their normal duties at South Road on 9th September. When Mr Adlem started his Headship of South Road in April, the place of Mr Hough (who had moved to Oakdale Junior School) was taken by Miss Alison Harding.

The new Head immediately agreed to sit on the steering committee for the Poole Teachers' Centre now set up in the old Drill Hall under the leadership of Mr A.J. Selwood. He seems not to have been very pleased with school lunch being served in the Family Service style, and after consultation with Mrs Gardiner, the school meals organiser, he re-introduced the Cafeteria system. Trouble was experienced with some suspect gravy soon after he had taken over, and he expressed surprise that this gravy did not affect the following day's attendance. All in all he was a little disillusioned with the meals. The PTA seems not to have been altogether acceptable to him for although they did organise fund raising events, he felt that the bulk of the hard work involved fell onto the staff.

In July of that first year of Mr Adlem's tenure, Miss Harding left to go to Canada. and Mr Green left to take up his appointment at Seldown School.

When the autumn term started on 9th September 1969, numbers at South Road had dropped to 207. The reason was that the new Canford Heath School had now opened and only 24 children from that area still remained at South Road School. The staff now was as follows :

Class 1	=	Mr W. Marshall
Class 2	=	Mr H. R. B. Francis
Class 3	=	Miss J. M. LeSueur
Class 4	=	Miss A. J. Punter
Class 5	=	Mrs G. N. Fagg
Class 6	=	Miss P. M. Brixey
Class 7	=	Mrs J. D. Ball (in charge of Infants)

Miss Anne Haysom was appointed Deputy Head of Dorchester Infants' School.

On November 26th with the NUT on strike it was necessary to close school for the morning. Again in 1970 from the end of January to 5th February school was closed on account of strike action by the NUT.

On a happier note, both the Netball and Football Teams were League Champions that year, and South Road won the B Section Championship at the Town Sports for the first time since 1931.

Miss LeSueur left to get married, and Miss Haysom took up her new appointment at the end of Mr Adlem's first year as Head.

It was in 1970 that the old Drill Hall adjacent to South Road School was completely taken over as a Teachers' Centre. With future development and road widening in mind it was agreed by the Education Committee to make purchase of even numbers 88 - 106 Green Road if they were put up for sale. The numbers 108 and 110 had already been purchased.

The necessity to provide some kind of pre-school age group activity was considered and the need for a Nursery Unit at South Road was acknowledged by the Borough Education Officer in 1971. As there was the requisite space available in the building, the idea was approved and the nursery unit set up as a result the following year still forms a very important part of the school, with the children attending half-day for one term or two, dependant upon their birth date in relation to the new school year. Strikes by members of the NUT now formed part of school life pattern and in June the strike was supported by 50 teachers in the area.

As from the Autumn term the supply of free milk was withdrawn, except to children up to seven years of age and special cases. From this date too, the practice was adopted of keeping Standard Record Cards and Standard Attainment Cards at school. The whole structure of schooling was in the process of being altered with the abolition of the selective system and all children would in future attend a First School from age 5-8, a Middle School 8-12, then follow on to an Upper School until the age of 16, when pupils requiring further advanced education would attend a 6th Form College.

With the advent of all the blocks of flats in the close proximity, South Road was now closed off and a new 9' high wire fence was erected around the boundaries of the school, which had for some years included the corner site of the old Butler's Brush Factory.

The enormous changeover that was in the melting pot during Mr Adlem's term of office meant that South Road County Primary School was scheduled to become a First School eventually, taking approximately 160 children of the ages 5-8, when they would pass over either to the Middle School planned for Garland Road or that which was being planned for Oakdale in Mellstock Road. In addition the school would house a Nursery Unit for about 40 children.

The interim arrangement was to be completed by September 1974 when South Road would be accommodating, in addition to the rising fives, children from 5 to 12 years of age, in other words a **Combined School.**

By this time Dorset Education Authority had taken over the decision-making, for the Poole Committee for Education had held their last meeting in March 1974. Under the local Government reorganisation on the 1st April 1974, Poole ceased to be an excepted District for Education.

Mr Adlem had to start to deal with the results of the Health and Safety at

Work Act 1974 and all that it entailed with regard to safety and fire precautions in the buildings had continuing effects for many years. The Bullock Report *"A Language for Life"* published in 1975 made quite clear that every school should have a co-ordinated policy for language teaching with the necessary staff and advisory back-up to implement it.

At this time too various parts of the County were operating, quite legally, three different Agreed Syllabuses of Religious Education. The new Dorset Education Committee decided that many of the assumptions made by the compilers of the 1948 Dorset Syllabus no longer applied and set out broad limits within which Religious Education in schools should now proceed. Strict guidelines were also set out by the Committee regarding heating and lighting in schools in view of the urgent need to save energy.

The Education Act of 1976 brought Comprehensive Education one step closer. The parents of the children attending the South Road Combined Schools were far from happy with the proposals that the children be sent out of the district for their education on attaining the age of eight to attend the Middle School planned for Oakdale.

It was on the 18th April 1977 that Mr Anthony N. Kellaway B.Ed. (Hons) commenced duties as Headmaster of South Road Combined School. He had previously been deputy and Acting Head of Hillbourne Middle School, Poole.

The Deputy Head of South Road was Mr W. Marshall with staff consisting of Mr D. Huxter, Mr H.R.B. Francis, Mr A. Cobb and Mrs A. Byron (Middle School Dept), together with Mrs J. Ball, Mrs S. Davey, Miss S. Harrison and Miss A. Merritt (First School Dept, including Nursery Unit). Mrs K. Kell and Mrs D. Christopher were part-time teachers. New member of staff, Mrs H. Parrell had been appointed to take charge of a newly created class of First School children accommodated at one end of the Main Hall. The number on the roll at this time was 298, which included 28 in the Nursery Unit.

Poole Teachers' Centre housed next door to School was by now being put to good use. The Great Debate on Education as launched by the Prime Minister was the subject of meetings held there during 1977 attended by all local Head teachers who were addressed by the County Education Officer, Mr Roy Price. During a French Course held there, children of the Middle School Department of South Road were used for demonstration purposes.

The new Head took his first opportunity to meet many of the parents at the PTA social evening held in the School Hall in May. Chairman of the Dorset Education Committee, Miss Jeanne Bisgood, visited school shortly afterwards and showed great interest in the Nursery Unit. The school received many callers during the early days of the new Head's reign. The Rector of St James' Parish Church, the Rev. John Potter, visited and also took Assembly at times.

Mr T. Moron, the teacher for Remedial Education, Miss J. Roberts (Adviser for Early Years) and PC Fowler, the local Police Liaison Officer, were also early visitors, as were Mrs Williams, tutor from the South Dorset Technical College, Weymouth; Miss R. Russell (Middle School Adviser); Area Education Officer, Mr Malcolm Bray; Mr Ward (Senior Advisor) and Mr Alexander, HM Inspector.

Keeping up the old tradition of the Maypole, the children of South Road gave a fine display of dancing when they joined other local First Schools in the Spring Festival of Song held at Hamworthy First School.

In this year of Jubilee, all the First School children visiting Poole Park on June 1st to picnic and visit the Zoo were dressed patriotically in red, white and blue.

The Nursery Unit enjoyed a treat later in June when they were taken by coach to Upton Park for a picnic tea and then a fine Jubilee Concert was held at St James Church in July combining the talents of South Road children with those from Alderney Middle School and Talbot Drive Combined School. This was enjoyed by the Mayor, local dignitaries and a church packed with people.

The July Camp at Carey, Wareham, continued to be part of the school tradition and Mr Kellaway visited the children there during the course of their stay. London and the Natural History and Science Museums at Kensington was the venue for the annual school outing.

Two of the staff, Mrs J. Ball (Head of First School Dept) and Miss S. Harrison left to take up appointments at the newly built Merley Combined School just before school broke up for the Summer holidays in 1977. Their places were taken by Mrs A. Bowyer and Miss S. Rogers in the new school year in September.

Cycling Proficiency classes were taken by Mr F. Watts and all the children participating passed the necessary test at the end of the course. Mr S. Stone of Bournemouth Drama Centre paid weekly visits to the school for Drama Coaching.

After the Harvest Festival Service in the school hall, the produce was distributed to the elderly of the neighbourhood by some of the older children. During the year a new Continental type barrier crossing had been installed in High Street to replace the old manually operated railway level crossing gates. A Safety Officer from British Rail visited all schools in the area to explain the workings of the new crossing barriers and the children of South Road went along to see them in operation in November. Also in November the older children, in preparation for their Secondary Education Selection, took two Verbal Reasoning Tests.

During this year and into 1978, the Headmaster and the managers spent many hours discussing the future aims and objects of the school, together with issues raised by the Great Debate on Education.

However, life still flowed its customary course at South Road and Christmas of 1977 was celebrated in the time honoured fashion of parties and Father Christmas's visit. The PTA Christmas Fair brought in just over £270 and the final Christmas assembly was led by the Rev. John Potter of St James Church.

The total number on the roll of the South Road Combined Primary School in January of 1978 was 269. This comprised 149 pupils in the Middle School, 95 in the First School and 25 in the Nursery.

Miss J. Glover started in the place of Mrs A. Bryon, who had left at the end of last year to take Maternity Leave and Mrs P. Turner started as Practical Assistant to the Middle School in place of Mr K. Cole. The third new face was that of Mrs J. Smith, who came to replace Mr D. Huxter, who was in very poor health. By February, with the onset of freezing cold weather, the tanker drivers went on strike with the consequence that no heating oil was delivered to school To help conserve stocks, school was closed at 3.30, but after heavy falls of snow mid-month, school was closed down and a rescue operation had to be carried out by a parent who could get through with his Land Rover to rescue the Nursery childrens' guinea-pigs, who were without food or water.

Mrs Pearce, the Canteen assistant who had worked at the school for 12 years, left in March and was replaced by Mrs Stanley. At around the same time the supervision of the school meals had to be undertaken by the Head and others of the staff to overcome the operation of sanctions by certain staff who were members of the NUT or NAS.

Many First School parents responded to an invitation to join the pupils for morning assembly and another innovation was the introduction of the new national May Day holiday.

In May 1978 Miss Glover married and became Mrs Leybourne. The First School children participated in a 'Sing-a-Long' at Poole Arts Centre and later demonstrated their Maypole Dancing skills in the school hall. A visit by Mr A. Tansley, authority on the teaching of reading, coincided with an Exhibition being held in the Teachers' Centre of books and apparatus used in the teaching of reading.

At a public meeting held in the school hall in June, discussion took place regarding the future pattern of schooling within the area. This meeting was chaired by Mr R. Hymers from County Hall and was packed to capacity. The parents present rejected the suggestion that children on reaching the age of eight years should transfer to the Middle School at Oakdale, leaving South Road as a First School for pupils of 3½ to 8 years of age. They insisted that the school retain its present format and continue to accommodate local children right through to the age of 12 years. The Nursery Unit caused a deal of interest and students from the Play Group Courses held at Bournemouth Technical College visited on occasions to observe it.

Both the First and Middle School Sports were held at the Seldown School grounds. During Carnival Week of 1978 an 'It's a Knock-Out' competition was held at Baiter and in the Carnival itself the school float, decorated on the theme of 'Multi-Coloured Swap Shop', was awarded the Grand Challenge Trophy as the outstanding float in 70 entries.

June 1978 Staff
Happy Staff Goup L to R. Mrs.Leybourne, Mrs. McPherson, Mrs. Turner, Mrs. Fallon,
Mrs. Parker (Secretary), Mr. Kellaway (Head), Mr. Francis, Mr. Marshall, Miss Merritt,
Mrs. Bowyer, Mrs Smith, Mrs. Davy, Mrs. Kell, Mr. Cobb.

One morning in July a group of French children from Cherbourg visited school and on the 15th July a farewell party was thrown for Mr Huxter, who had retired on a 'breakdown pension'. Just before school broke up for the Summer holidays, the Head and Deputy Head took a party of Middle School senior children to London on an outing and the following day a junior band from the Poole Grammar School visited and gave a concert to the whole of South Road.

Both Mrs Smith and Mrs Leybourne left at the end of term and when the new term started in September, Mrs Cotgrove joined the staff, together with Mr R. Davis from the Talbot Combined School, who had accepted the post of Language Development teacher. The number on the roll now stood at 240. To enable school meals to be served more quickly and quietly, individual trays were introduced.

The PTA was still very active and fund-raising events were organised throughout the year, including a Jumble Sale in October which raised £70. Later the Christmas Fair brought in £295 and enabled the PTA to donate £150 towards the cost of supplying the school hall with fully lined curtains, which were hung just in time for the Christmas festivities.

The annual Cycling Proficiency Contest was held in October around selected roads in the Borough and in the same month the children of both schools visited the Central Library on separate occasions to see an Exhibition of Library Books. Aspects of the Health and Safety at Work Act were still being discussed at length by all Heads in the area and these meetings were held at the Teachers' Centre adjacent to South Road.

Just before the half term break, Miss Cooper, the NNEB (National Nursery Education Board) assistant in the Nursery Unit married and became Mrs Fallon.

The Hall, festooned with Christmas decorations and decked in the new curtains was a fit setting for the social evening arranged by the PTA as a farewell gesture to Mr W. Marshall, the Deputy Head, who had served the school for 29 years. During the evening he was presented with a cheque by the Chairman of the PTA, Mr L. Coombes, on behalf of parents and past pupils. Over one hundred visitors attended including the Chairman of Dorset Education Committee, Miss Jeanne Bisgood and the Area Education Officer, Mr Malcolm Bray.

The Staff organised another social evening for Mr Marshall at which three ex-Heads attended. They were Mr Lee Hartnell, Mr B. Goodman and Mr R. Adlem. Mr Goodman presented Mr Marshall with a stereo record player on behalf of the guests. Yet another presentation was made from the children at the closing assembly on December 20th.

When school re-commenced at the start of 1979, Mr S. Bridges became the Deputy Head. The number on the roll stood at 238 and during the whole of this year the school participated in a research project to study 'Transition and Continuity in early Education'. South Road was one of only eight units countrywide involved in this NFER (National Foundation for Educational Research) project.

In February and in deference to the Health and Safety at Work Act, independent fire alarm gongs were fitted in the main school, two upstairs and two down, so that in the event of a main bell circuit failure, the alarm could be sounded.

The school was situated within the Green Road/Emerson Road General Improvement Area and plans for enhancing the environment were set out by a deputation which visited school. Mr Kellaway greeted representatives from the Borough Council headed by the Environmental Health Officer and this resulted later in a Public Meeting of local residents to discuss plans for reorganisation of the road system in the immediate area.

The PTA arranged and financed a performance by the Ballet-Go-Round Company of *"The Performing World of Animals"* which was much enjoyed in February. Then on March 23rd 1979 the South Road children took their places along a section of High Street where Her Majesty, Queen Elizabeth II and HRH Prince Philip were to travel during their day visit to Poole. All the children carried a Union Flag and one of the First School was able to present Her Majesty with a posy of flowers.

In April it was the Yellow House which carried off both the Football and the Netball Inter-House matches.

The managers had requested that a gate be erected across the entrance to the children's playground to curtail excess parking in the playground during

Thanks mainly to the efforts of J N Simon Bridges, the walled area at the far end of the playground was transformed into a nature area. Here, in 1982 the top class are helping to put the finishing touches to the pond.

school hours. This was now carried out.

During the term, parents of the First School scholars joined them one morning at assembly. Final assembly was conducted by the Rector of St James', the Revd. Potter.

During the summer term, the Middle School Sports held at the Seldown School playing fields was won by Green House. The trophy was presented by the recently retired Mr Marshall. The school's prize-winning Float at Poole Carnival *"Hey look, that's me"* was to lead to an exciting event. On 8th December the children travelled to the Mayflower Park at Southampton to be filmed for a programme of *"Hey look, that's me"*. (This was subsequently televised on BBC-TV on February 5th, 1980.)

At the final assembly the Chairman of the Managers, Mr W.S. Rigler and the Schools' Police Liaison Officer (P.E. Beale) attended to witness Mr A. Wills, a past pupil, present the Challenge Cup and Music Trophy he had donated to the Yellow House and a fourth year pupil.

After the Summer holidays, Miss J. Manson, B Ed. and Mrs C. Labouchardiere joined the teaching force, Mrs Davey having commenced maternity leave and the Practical Assistant in the Middle School Mrs Turner, having left in June.

A term's Drama course for 2 classes was started by Mr S. Stone, a Peripatetic teacher from Bournemouth Drama Centre. The school played host

Nursey Class 1983

| Miss Cavell | Mrs La Bouchardiere | Nursey Student |
| Richard Baxter | Tara Moore | James Bolton | John Matthews |

| Sara Peckham | Stephen Wood | Rhea Vine | Elizabeth Hall | Amy Bale | Adam Ramsbotham | Fiona Grimshaw |

on September 19th to a group of Vietnamese refugee children who visited from the Camp at Sopley, where they were being housed temporarily. Accompanying them was a former Nursery Class teacher, Miss A. Merritt.

Weekly swimming lessons were taken by some of the Middle School children at the Dolphin Swimming Pool in Kingland Road. The cost was borne by the parents.

The new Conservative Government elected in May 1979 under the first woman Prime Minister, Mrs Margaret Thatcher, had decreed that expenditure must be cut. On this directive from Central Government, the County Education Officer and the Chairman of the Education Committee called a meeting for Heads of the area to attend at the Parkstone Grammar School on October 11th. There they discussed various means whereby Education expenditure could be reduced without impairing basic teaching. This new Government realised that a new agreed framework for essential education in Primary and Secondary schools should be worked out by the local Education authorities and the teaching staff. It was suggested that there was need for extensions in the teaching of English and Literature,

Mathematics, science and modern languages. The instruction of Religion was also in need of review. The Government intended to remove the requirement for local Education Authorities to submit plans for the re-organisation of secondary schools on comprehensive lines. This changeover to the Comprehensive system had been due to start in 1981 (Year I) and progress systematically through years II, III, IV and V and be completed in 1985. Meetings at South Road had shown that parents in the area would be well pleased if these proposals were not carried through and so with the dawn of 1980, it seemed that for the time being at least, South Road would stay as a Combined School.

Mr Kellaway continued to encourage the children to participate in extra-curriculum subjects. The staff and the parents shared a special kind of relationship which encouraged an active and helpful Parent-Teacher Association. For example, at the end of October of 1979 when the PTA held their AGM., the children gave a little concert with choir, recorder players and playlets acted in French. The Christmas Fayre held on November 23rd raised the grand sum of £315.

At the close of 1979, the Headmaster submitted the findings of the year's Research Project to the Headquarters of the National Foundation for Educational Research. In addition, he sent his own report to County Hall.

The Staff at that time was as follows: Mr A. N. Kellaway, B Ed. Hons (Headmaster), Mr S. Bridges (Deputy Headmaster), Mrs A. Bowyer, B Ed. (Head of First School Dept), *Middle Years*: Mr S. Bridges (Class M), Mr R. Davis, B Ed. Hons (Class M[E]), Mrs S. McPherson (Class 1), Mr H. R. B. Francis (Class 2), Mrs J. Kell (Class 3), *First School*: Miss J. Manson, B Ed. (Class 4), Mr A. J. Cobb (Class 5), Mrs C. Labouchardiere (Class 6), Mrs A. Bowyer, B Ed. (Nursery Class), Mrs N. Fallon, NNEB (Nursery Assistant), *Part-Time Staff*: Mrs A. Cotgrove (H.E. and Needlecraft), Mrs D. Christopher (Music), Mr K. de Souza (French), Mrs J. M. Parker (School Secretary), Mr C. Bridges (School Caretaker), Mrs J. M. Craig (First School Auxiliary), *School Managers*: Mr W.S. Rigler (Chairman), Mr P. Anderson (Parent Representative). The school uniform colours were Royal blue and white.

The dawn of the 1980's may have held many uncertainties but as 1979 drew to a close, South Road School played out its role in the time-honoured way. School was decorated through-out in the theme of *'The Twelve Days of Christmas'*. The Middle School held a carol concert at the Arts Centre and raised enough money to purchase food from the then Safeway shop in the then Arndale Centre. This was parcelled up in Christmas wrappings for distribution by some of the older children to the old folk of Poole. First School children held their carol concert in front of a packed audience and raised in excess of £20. An old tradition of hiding money in the Christmas Pudding was revived and at the School Christmas lunch, everyone was hoping for a 'lucky' helping. The school parties were much enjoyed by all, the older children holding a 'Disco' and, of course, Father Christmas made his usual appearance. Again too, the children were puzzled and entertained by Freddie Bale, the magician. School broke up on Wednesday December 19th. Final

Assembly taken in the Hall was still in the spirit of Christmas for the decorations were kept up until the children had departed.

When school re-commenced on 8th January 1980 a few troubles surfaced. The Road Crossing patrol lady (Mrs Robins) was unfit for duty and parents had to be informed by letter to make arrangements for their children to be brought and collected from school. No sooner was Mrs Robins back on duty than the ceiling in the Boiler house collapsed due to a leaking flat roof which had not been re-surfaced. Later that month the cost of school dinners went up to 35p per day. It appears that head lice were still a problem and every child was examined. Parents were invited to view films concerning the problem. Such film shows highlighting various aspects of school life became a regular feature.

In March the 4th year children performed a musical play *"Mrs Noah is missing"* to old folk in the Moose Hall at Jolliffe Road in the presence of the Mayor. Also that month twelve French children who were spending a week-end in local homes visited the school. These exchanges were encouraged to help the children with their French. By April the Borough Works Department had begun work on 110 Green Road in readiness for occupation by the school caretaker.

A grand old custom of Maypole Dancing was continued. This year a public performance at Upton House was so well received that it was suggested it became an annual event. In June the Annual Town Sports were held at Seldown School (now demolished) and 4th year boy Gavin Wright won the High Jump Event.

In July, the first *"South Road Chronicle"* since 1938 went on sale at a price of 15p. This was another custom to be repeated every year. On July 22nd a farewell party was held for Mr H.R.B. Francis on his retirement after 34 years faithful service at South Road. The Staff presented him with a radio to enjoy in his retirement. Past Headmasters, Lee Hartnell, Mr B. Goodman and Mr R. Adlem all attended together with past deputy head, Mr W. Marshall.

When school re-opened after the summer holidays Miss Charlotte Barr and Mrs Sally Hall joined the staff, and in November the Headmaster, accompanied by eight Senior children, attended the ceremony of the granting of the Freedom of the Borough to Mr W.S.("Bill") Rigler, Chairman of the School Governors. He was later awarded the M.B.E. and attended the official presentation by HM Queen Elizabeth II. In March of the following year, Mr Andrew Hawkes (whose Grandfather, Councillor J.A. Hawkes had performed the opening ceremony of South Road in 1912) became a Parent Representative. The School Secretary, Mrs J. Parker retired after 12 years' service. She was presented with an electric hot-plate from the children and later with a Royal Doulton Dinner Service by the Staff.

On the 24th July the Reverend John Potter led the final assembly. Then First and Middle Schools held separate assemblies for the distribution of certificates and cups. The new 'Young Award' was introduced for the best contribution to the School Magazine as chosen by Mrs D.E.W. Young, following the author's

Staff Pantomime 1984
Standing: Marjorie Longden, Tony Kellaway (Headmaster), Mrs Brown, Mr Bridges,
Mr Byant, Charlotte Thompson.
Seated: Mr Cobb, Miss Vye.

original publication of her book *"Schools of Old Poole"* which centred around South Road School. The first award was won by Kate Fletcher.

Once again in November, the children aged 12+ participated in a Verbal Reasoning Test which had become part of the selection procedure for entry to the Grammar Schools.

In March of 1982 the Wedding of Prince Charles to Lady Diana Spencer was marked by the children of the First School planting trees, under the guidance of the Poole Parks' Department, in the grassed area at the end of the playground.

On the last day of March at 7.30 p.m. the school telephone number was officially changed, as were all Poole numbers, by adding the prefix 6, thus making it 673966 The next day, April 1st, saw many children up at the crack of dawn looking for the arrival of the 'Phoenix Bird' which, they had learned, showed up only once every 500 years!

Some Middle School pupils took part in a series of English Tests devised by the NFER as a research project. Mrs C. Brown took up duties as School Secretary the same day that a group of children went down to the Quay to visit *HMS Bildeston* which was making a courtesy call to Poole. This was particularly enjoyed because most of HM Naval force were engaged in the Falklands conflict.

In September the school re-opened with staff as follows:- Mr A. Kellaway Headmaster, Mr S. Bridges Deputy Headmaster, Mr D. Evans, Mrs C. Kirkham, Mr A. Cobb, Miss C. Barr , Mrs J. Kell, Mrs C. Labouchardiere, Mrs P. Hackforth. Total number on Roll - 172 children

Other Staff: Mrs S. Hall, H.E. and Remedial, Mrs E. Irvine, Music (new appointment), Mrs Dodman, French (new appointment)

By the beginning of 1983 it was deemed necessary to investigate the possibility of installing a burglar alarm system into school and this was duly implemented in September. It was later connected direct to the Police Station but was not without its pitfalls for on several occasions, and usually at night, it activated in response to thunderstorms, and once to incorrect setting by a temporary Caretaker taken on at short notice.

The two top years entered the Triangular Athletics Match (an annual event) held at Seldown School in June and brought honour to South Road by gaining second place.

The spare plot of ground at the far end of the playground had by now been designated a Nature Area and Mr Simon Bridges' idea of building a pond there now came to fruition. The parents worked hard to help turn this area into a picnic site where the children could enjoy pond and plant life. A large block of Purbeck stone was collected from Langton Matravers for a sundial plinth which, on the optimum date of mid-Summer day in 1984 was set to read Greenwich Mean Time. This garden was to be featured several times over the years in the local newspapers.

The highlight of that year was the visit by HM Queen Elizabeth II on 27th June to the Royal Marines' Camp at Hamworthy. All the school children with the exception of Jehovah Witnesses, lined the pavements in West Quay Road to welcome her.

January 1985 saw a very heavy fall of snow which prevented some staff and pupils from attending. Not surprisingly, the swimming lessons had to be cancelled. The children continued to enjoy a wide range of activities outside school. They visited the Towngate Theatre, Hengistbury Head, Corfe Castle, the Maritime Museum and the Mayor's Parlour, attended concerts by the Bournemouth Symphony Orchestra and took Cycling Proficiency Tests. The PTA were as usual active with Treasure Hunts, Car Boot Sales and Barn Dances.

Before breaking for Summer Holidays the teaching staff cleared all cupboards and classrooms in preparation for the installation of a new heating system together with a complete re-wiring of the whole school.

Industrial strife hit the school in support of the Teachers' Union Pay Claim. On October 1st classes were sadly disrupted but the next day the Harvest Festival Service was fully attended at St James Church.

July 1986
School entrance doors daubed with 'blood' by Animal Liberation Movement.

Work on the new heating and electrical system progressed so slowly that the re-opening of school term after the Summer break had to be delayed for a week. Even then the workmen were still there making life a bit difficult for all concerned until the end of the year.

At the beginning of 1986 a new carpet was laid in the entrance hall, the newly installed fire alarm and lighting systems were commissioned and the lighting computer programmed. In March the restoration of Scaplen's Court was discussed with a view to providing facilities to enable children of the Borough to use it for study purposes. The transformation of Scaplen's Court for the benefit of school children made rapid progress. Even the old kitchen was used for cooking using the open ranges and fire. It also became a popular venue for children to entertain the elderly folk from the Old Town and share the results of their cooking labours with them.

When two School Inspectors paid an Informal Visit in July they attended a variety of lessons and were impressed by the strong work ethic at South Road. Headmaster Mr Kellaway was congratulated for the highly organised and professional attitude which was evident in all areas of the school.

Unfortunately, later that month the Animal Liberation Front felt obliged to daub the main school entrance doors with red paint. It was assumed they were protesting against the use of the school as a meeting place for the local branch of Dorset Young Farmers.

On July 23rd, the children, encouraged to wear 'wedding clothes', were allowed to watch on TV the wedding of HRH Prince Andrew to Sarah Ferguson. A pleasant end to term.

When the Autumn Term commenced the staff were: Mr A. Kellaway

(Headmaster), Mr S. Bridges (Deputy Headmaster), Mrs C. Labouchardiere, Mrs S. Hall, H.E., Mrs J. Kell, Mrs A. Lloyd, Music, Miss E. Vye, Mrs C. Brown (Secretary), Mr A. Cobb, Mrs M. Longden (Welfare Assistant), Mrs C. Thompson, Miss Y. Cavell (Nursery Assistant) Miss S. Whitehall, Mr & Mrs D. Whitbread (Caretaker & Cleaner). Later in the month Madame Regine Chlubek joined the staff as a teacher of French.

Towards the end of 1986 much thought was given to the preparation of events to celebrate the Schools 75th Anniversary in January of 1987. A special 75th Anniversary Chronicle was produced. The actual anniversary date, January 5th, was the last day of the Christmas Holiday and so the 15th was chosen as the official day to open the School to all pupils and ex-pupils from far afield. A heavy snowfall prevented some from attending, but Mr C. Lee Hartnell braved the elements to be welcomed as guest of honour by the Town Crier, Mr Malcolm Squires (an ex-pupil). In the Hall exhibitions had been mounted which included a collection of H.P. Smith's artefacts, photos, flower arrangements and flags arranged by the RNLI, also an up-to-date list of 'Young Award' winners. The 8 year old great-great grandson of Alderman Hawkes, who opened the school in 1912, unveiled a commemorative plaque. Present day pupils were happy to show those present around the school and apparently many elderly gentlemen were delighted at last to be allowed upstairs where, in the early days, only females were allowed. A video film, commemorative mugs, book markers and diaries recorded the occasion and the 1981 book *"Schools of Old Poole"* was displayed for reference.

The following week the happy occasion continued with a Music Hall

Concert given by the staff and some pupils who had enjoyed learning some of the old music hall songs. Word of the Anniversary had spread and for weeks the school received messages of congratulations from all over the world including a telegram from America!

And then on the 17th February an Anniversary Thanksgiving Service was held at the Parish Church of St James. Sam Rockett, the ex-South Road boy of Channel swimming fame read the lesson. The service was well attended and included the rendering of a William Knapp hymn by a quartet of teaching staff.

At the end of June school closed for the last 'Occasional Days'. In future, they were to be known as 'Staff Days' to be used for staff training whilst the children were on holiday. In order to comply with the 1986 Education Act, the first of the Annual Meetings for Parents was held on July 22nd attended by the School Governors and four parents!

A memorable year drew to a happy close with parties and Christmas entertainment.

By 1988, because Newfoundland Way from Baiter had been extended, the positioning of the pedestrian crossing into Lagland Street was causing concern. South Road children had conducted their own traffic survey and this resulted in the council moving the crossing a safer distance from the existing roundabout.

A PTA Superschools Event raised funds to replace P.E. apparatus when Hayley Price, international gymnast came to school and demonstrated her skills. The School Secretary Mrs Caroline Brown left for another job.

It was around this time that plans emerged to re-name Henry Harbin School. At this time adding Technical High was all that was suggested, but it later emerged as Poole High. There was strong local feeling that the Henry Harbin name be perpetuated in memory of his great benevolence to schooling, not least the Harbin Trust which had funded Prizes to school children in Poole for many years.

The children continued to enjoy many ex-curricular activities and in May of 1988 accompanied by the Deputy Head and Miss Vye some 3rd and 4th years spent a week in Wales participating in Archery, Pony Trekking, climbing and canoeing. An educational visit was paid the next week to Marwell Zoo near Winchester. This visit led to a project by the children to sponsor the upkeep of a Rhea and by holding book and cake sales they raised the sum of £70.

Then on 21 June an enormous explosion, followed by fire occurred at the BDH - British Drug Houses - premises in West Quay Road. (Since renamed Merck after its German parent company). The whole town was shocked by the severity of the explosion which caused damage to nearby properties including the Queen Mary pub alongside and the Link House Publications' building opposite. In the interests of safety people from a wide area were rapidly evacuated from their homes and many who were without family or friends nearby spent the night in the Arts Centre. Miraculously no-one was

Staff June 1990
Back row: Mrs Lloyd, Miss Vye, Mr Palmer (Caretaker), Miss Carter (Secretary), Miss Cavell (Nursey Assistant NNEB), Mrs Downer, Mrs La Bouchardiere and Mrs Whish.
Front Row: Mrs Hall, Mrs Kell, Mr Adams (Deputy Head, Stanley Green), Mr Kellaway (Headmaster), Mr Bridges, Mr Cobb and Mrs Longen.

injured, just badly shaken and next day it was no surprise that school attendance was low. However, the Nursery children were escorted, as planned, on their trip to Moors Valley Park Farm.

Fifteen Spanish teachers visited South Road in July and seemed amazed at the range of activities involved.

When the Autumn Term commenced the staff were as follows: Mr A. Kellaway (Headmaster), Mr S. Bridges (Deputy Headmaster), Mrs C. Thompson, Miss S. Whitehall, Mrs J. Kell, Mrs C. Labouchardiere, Miss E. Vye, Mrs S. Hall (H.E.), Mr A. Cobb, Mrs A. Lloyd (Music), Mrs J. McBride' Mrs J. Downer, Mrs M. Longden (Welfare Assistant), Miss Y. Cavell (Nursery Assistant)

HRH The Princess of Wales, Princess Diana, visited Poole on 14 September to celebrate the 10th Anniversary of the opening of Poole Arts Centre. Several children were given permission to attend. And the same week the choir gave a concert at Scaplen's Court as part of the Flower Festival Celebrations.

Although not implemented until April 1990, Local Management of

Schools (LMS), was discussed at the end of 1988 by the Local Education Authority. 'Teaching Appraisal' was another proposal put forward by the Education Minister Mr Kenneth Baker which needed to be discussed thoroughly. A version of this and 'payment by results' had both been features of nineteenth century education. A more welcome new venture was the teaching of Craft, Design & Technology (CDT) for which purpose a room in the former Teachers' Centre had been converted.

Not wearing school uniform for a day proved a popular means of raising funds for 'Children in Need' appeal. For the privilege of turning up to school in whatever took their fancy the children each donated at least 20p. This ruse was to be repeated on future occasions to raise money for various charities such as 'Comic Relief.'

The Annual Christmas Concerts at the Arts Centre were always well attended by relatives and friends and 1988 was no exception. South Road Choir and Recorders joined with other local Middle and Secondary schools to provide a rousing evening's entertainment. The choir also led the carol singing during the Christmas Carol Concert held from the steps of the Guildhall in Market Street, accompanied by Poole Silver Band. The Deputy Mayor, Councillor R. Meech conducted the proceedings.

The new 'Waterfront' Museum at the bottom end of the High Street near the Quay was shortly to open teaching facilities available to those schools applying for group membership. This was done on behalf of South Road.

The forthcoming implementation in September 1989 of the new National Curriculum in a range of subjects including Maths, English, French, Health Education and Science resulted in various out-of-school meetings for the staff concerned and a certain amount of opposition from the Governing Body. Then national concern regarding safety of school children in playgrounds became a controversial issue at South Road. Two sets of bars in the play area which had been in constant use for 50 years without incident had to be removed because the Governors deemed the risk of injury too great. The move was not popular with the children. Compensation of sorts came when a PE climbing frame and ropes were fitted into the main hall; these having been removed from the St Peter's Middle School on its closure. South Road staff were given a demonstration of this newly installed apparatus by Mr T. Hall the PE teacher from Poole Grammar School.

When the top three classes attended the orchestral concert by the BSO this year, the cost of transport, amounting to £70, was for the first time met by the parents since the Education Reform Act of 1988 forbade the charging of such costs to school budgets.

The Borough Council held a public meeting in the school hall to explain how the new Poll Tax was to be implemented when it replaced the centuries-old rating system. In the event there was so much opposition that Poll Tax was eventually scrapped and a banded system of charge based on property was introduced, known as Community Charge, from which expenditure on local services, including education, supported by Exchequer grant, was to be met, but which was subject, like its predecessor, to strict Government capping controls.

It was with great pride that South Road received trophies and cheques to the value of £95 from Poole Maritime Trust for its successful entry into the Museum's Annual competition. The cash was spent on library books and craft equipment for use in a recently converted room in the former Teachers' Centre. Meech's Forge, as it had been renamed, was soon however to be evacuated until necessary Fire Precaution work could be carried out.

Staff were changing, for Mrs McBride and Miss Whitehall both left in July and when School re-opened after the Summer Holidays, the staff, in accordance with National Curriculum guidelines, were as follows: Mrs Labouchardiere (Year 0 - Nursery), Mrs Davey (Year 1, 5-6 Yrs), Mr Adams (Year 2, 6-7 Yrs), Mrs Hall (Year 3, 7-8 Yrs), Mrs Whish (Year 4, 8-9 Yrs), Miss Vye (Year 5, 9-10 Yrs), Mrs Kell (Year 6, 10-11 Yrs), Mr Cobb (Year 7, 11-12 Yrs).

Mr Bridges (Deputy Head) specialised in the teaching of Science and Technology; Mrs Lloyd, Music and Home Economics and Mrs Downer (part-time) in Special Educational Needs. Keystages I and III of Maths and Science were commenced as was Keystage I of English as decreed by the Government's introduction of a National Curriculum. These areas of the curriculum were known as Core subjects and together with R.E. and other Foundation subjects composed the majority of the curriculum to be taught forthwith.

The National Curriculum necessitated the adoption of a more rigidly structured timetable and the Governors were called upon to meet more regularly to help deal with the situation. Parents of children in Years 1, 2 and 3 were given the opportunity to work alongside their children and to talk with the staff over the new regime.

Children in Year 7, to obtain a place at Grammar School, were now obliged to sit a battery of three selection tests, each approximately 50 minutes' duration. The first, a Verbal Reasoning Test, the second, on another day, an English Test, finally a Maths test. An average score of 120.5 on all three papers had to be reached.

Gold necklaces were found in the playground just before Christmas and after the police had been informed it was discovered that they had been stolen during the night from the Argos store in the Dolphin Centre (as the Arndale Centre had been renamed after a change of ownership).

A highlight at the end of 1989 was the visit by HRH The Princess Anne to Poole to join in commemorating the work of the Missions to Seamen. Twenty children from South Road attended the Church Service at St James' together with Mr Kellaway and Mrs Lloyd. Everyone was delighted to have been allocated seats with a good view of the Princess as she read the lesson.

A flu epidemic very nearly caused the cancellation of the annual Christmas entertainment to the parents. However a reduced cast carried on and were, as always well received. Again rain dampened the choir as they sang carols on the Guildhall Steps to the accompaniment of Poole Borough Band. In the New Year storm force winds created havoc over the entire country. Trees were uprooted, and such was the storm that it was considered necessary to evacuate the mobile classroom and cancel playtimes due to the danger of flying debris. Several of the smaller children were literally blown over in the playground getting into school.

'Book Week' took place in early March when a Book Fair, Puppet show, plays, writing, story readings and such-like activities took over from the normal school timetable. George Blake gave a slide show entitled *"Slides of Old Poole"* to the PTA one evening. Being an Old Poole man, he proved well equipped to supply the running commentary accompanying the pictures. Scaplen's Court was again used in a County Research Project encompassing artists, musicians and dancers. To follow on from this some of the children attended a performance of *Giselle* at the Poole Arts Centre.

Mrs Labouchardiere retired in July and when school re-convened after the Summer Break, the staff were as follows: Mr A. Kellaway (Headmaster), Mr S. Bridges (Deputy Headmaster), Mr C. Adams (Year 1/2), Mrs C. Oliver (Year R/1), Mr A. Cobb (Year 7), Mrs S. Davey (Nursery), Mrs J. Kell (Year 6), Mrs A. Lloyd (Music/H.E.), Miss E. Vye (Year 5), Mrs J. Downer (part-time – Remedial), Mrs C. Whish (Year 4), Miss Y. Cavell (Nursery Assistant), Mrs S. Hall (Year 2/3), Mrs L. Carter (Secretary).

It was now that the first indication came that South Road School was to be closed and Middle School children transferred to a newly built Middle school. It was planned that the South Road building would be designated a First School only.

As the Headmaster, Mr Kellaway wrote in his Log Book on 17 September 1990 *"In some ways it was a sad decision, but if the middle school children of the town were to be given every opportunity with their schooling in the 21st century then more suitable buildings must be provided - an impossibility on the present site. Many parents and governors opposed the proposition"*. By October the Dorset Education Committee had ratified the eventual closure of South Road as and when the new replacement Middle School was built. This was then expected to be in 1995.

The sad death of an ex-pupil due to a road accident was mourned and the Head and Deputy attended the funeral of Belinda Smith. Another former pupil, Matthew Anderson, met with an horrific accident in Canada and was expected to be paralysed from the neck down for life. A fund was set up for him and a collection taken at the Christmas Church Service at St James', and a non-uniform day at school, plus the proceeds from a Five-a-Side football tournament were sent to his family.

Troubles never come singly, for shortly after that accident, Claire Foster-Smith, her mother and grandmother were killed on their way to visit relatives in Leeds. Her sister, Naomi, also a pupil, was only slightly injured. In the New Year a commemorative tree was planted in the Nature Area.

Just before Christmas HM Inspector Mr Peter Dougill visited and showed

1991 Nursery Group with Miss Cavell and Mrs Davey.

particular interest in the English curriculum which he found satisfactory in every way.

For once the evening Christmas Carol Service on the Guildhall Steps was conducted in fine dry weather. Accompanied by Poole Silver Band and the Wareham Handbell Ringers, the evening was a great success. The Christmas Charity at School for Romanian Orphans was sponsored by a Bring & Buy Sale and raised £58.

The recently introduced Standard Attainment Tests (SAT's)were put into practice after Easter of 1991 together with the implementation of the National Curriculum, all of which consumed a great deal of staff time. Local Management of Schools also came into effect whereby the Governors, through the Headteacher, became responsible for the major financing within the school. This encompassed the employment and dismissal of staff. Later that year, one of the school governors, Edward 'Tom' Churchill, who was Sheriff of Poole, died.

In July the County Archivist, Mr Hugh Jacques, collected for safe keeping all the old South Road School Log Books and also those of the National School, and Lagland Street. By September the school had been completely re-decorated both externally (in blue and white) and internally, together with new Forms F2 and F3. The Rector of St James' the Revd

1991 Mr Cobb with top class in uniform.

Stanley Holbrook-Jones resigned as a Governor of the School.

Fund raising activities really took off just before Christmas 1991. They included a donation to St John's Ambulance Brigade, following a PE workout with Todd Bennett the Olympic athlete and £900 was raised by a PTA evening concert featuring a saxophone quartet from the Instrumental Music Service. Then £120 was donated to the Salvation Army's 'Crisis at Christmas' Appeal.

In May, the Royal Marines (based at Hamworthy) exercised their right as Freemen of the Borough to march through the streets of Poole. It was a proud and moving sight which all the children were allowed to watch from Lagland Street. Implementing LMS had necessitated the installation of additional modern equipment, and a keyboard, monitor and computer printer were set up in the Headteacher's office. The Grammar Schools at this time had acquired Grant Maintained Status (GMS). By October of 1992 the expectation was that as early as September 1995, the Tatnam Farm site would be operational and that South Road would be converted to a First School.

With all the recent changes in educational policies and the uncertainties over the future of South Road, staff morale reached a new low and a favourable Inspectors' report, indicating a well ordered, happy and caring community, came as a welcome boost in October 1992. That year for the first time, parents had the right to withdraw their Year 7 children from the Verbal Reasoning Test (VRT) in preparation for selection to Grammar Schools and two families exercised that right.

In January 1993 the Poole Town Community Centre commenced a block booking of South Road School Dining Hall to hold events whilst their own premises in Lagland Street – formerly Lagland Street Boys' Club – were being re-decorated. Use of the hall, free of charge, was also allowed for Poole Borough Housing Department to hold a party for children of homeless parents.

On 3rd February 1993 the children and staff walked along to Holes Bay Road to watch, at a safe distance, the demolition of Poole Power Station chimneys. This was the start of the total demolition of the Power Station following its de-commissioning.

Great excitement followed in April when children in the Nursery helped a Channel 4 Television unit film an *"Equinox"* programme on 'Memory'. It was shown on 31st October. Also that month, two Class 7 children represented school at the 'Beating the Bounds' ceremony organised from time to time by the Society of Poole Men from the Quay.

The Staff Training Day in July was held at Heathlands Hotel, Bournemouth and was committed to discussing Teacher Appraisal. Later in the year a two day residential course, held at Portland Heights Hotel, dealt with Headteacher Appraisal.

Just before Christmas the Headteacher, Mr Kellaway, was called out in the middle of the night to investigate the activation of the intruder alarm at South Road. On entering the building he apprehended the offending 'Cat Burglar' who had been inadvertently locked in – complete with 4 legs, a tail and a sleek tabby fur coat!

The usual round of Carol Services and Christmas parties by children, staff and parents brought the year to a close and the New Year of 1994 brought the disappointing news that due to legal matters the building of the new Tatnam Farm School was to be postponed until 1997.

In March, the forthcoming 50th Anniversary of D-Day (6th June 1944), was celebrated by the Society of Poole Men in the School Hall. The annual H.P. Smith Memorial Lecture given by Mr Ian Andrews, ex-Town Clerk of Poole, previewed his publication for Poole Historical Trust on Poole's role and on the actual D-day Anniversary a special assembly was held at school.

Then at last, before school broke up for the Summer recess, plans were available for the new Tatnam Farm Middle School. These were displayed at a PTA meeting held to view a video made during an Arts' Week of the children's efforts in painting, dance, drama and music. In conjunction with other schools in the Poole Technical High catchment area their work had been displayed in the Longfleet Gallery of Poole Arts Centre.

By September of 1994 the staff was as follows: Mr Kellaway (Headmaster), Mr Bridges (Deputy Headmaster), Mrs L. Carter, Mrs C.

July 1994, Children being entertained during Arts Week.

Boulton , Mr A. Cobb, Mrs S. Davey, Mrs S. Hall, Miss Y. Cavell, Miss E. Vye, Mrs M. Longden, Mrs C. Whish, Mrs L. Lowe, Miss T. Ligema, Mr R. Palmer (Caretaker), Mrs A. Barton, Mrs C. Oliver, Mrs A. Lloyd (Part-time), Mrs J. Downer (Part-time).

A new method of secondary selection came into practice at this time whereby the onus to put forward pupils for Grammar School entry was placed on the parents.

The School participated in the Nationwide Cancer Relief MacMillan Fund coffee morning which qualified for an entry into the Guinness Book of Records. South Road's contribution was £105.

One of the main entrance gates and part of the railings had to be removed temporarily to make room for a large mobile crane which hoisted the three sections of the new mobile classroom over the Staff room roof ready for positioning next to the existing mobile. It came into use after the Christmas break.

The school was delighted when Mrs Myrna Chave from Guide Dogs for the Blind attended in February to present them with a framed photograph of the dog *(Prince)* they had sponsored following her earlier visit with a blind person and his dog. At the end of term Assembly in April the PTA organised a raffle for Easter Eggs. Congratulations were extended to Thomas O'Sullivan who had brought honour to South Road on his selection to the Under 11's England Squad for Karate.

1994, The nature area is now fully developed. The trees have matured. The pond is stocked with fish and plants. A sundial and bird table have been installed. A perfect place to picnic!

For the first time in April of 1995 the school midday meals were delivererd in a refrigerated van, having been prepared in Bristol and driven down overnight.

The VE Day 50th Anniversary was celebrated on 5th May in the playground, which was set up as a War-Time 'Street Party' with the children dressed in the style of the 1940's. A collection was made for the British Legion. On the following Sunday the Headmaster, as representative of the school, attended a VE Day Service in St James Church.

Standard Assessment Tests were introduced in May for children in Year 6 at the end of Key Stage II. These referred to Maths, English and Science and were compulsory. It was necessary for the published results to be sent to parents at a later date.

Because the life of South Road School as the people of Poole had known it over the years was due to be over in 1997, when the new Tatnam Farm Middle School is completed, an aerial photograph *(see front cover)* was commissioned to capture it for posterity in its original site and, in the main, its original form.

The weather was exceptionally fine and sunny throughout the Summer of 1995 which made trips by various classes even more enjoyable than usual. These included Carey Camp for River study, the Arts' Day at Kingston Lacy

House, Wimborne, Marwell Zoo, 'The Alice in Wonderland' Maze at Bournemouth and the replica of the *Golden Hind* sailing ship at Poole Quay. The children also visited Brownsea Island, Putlake Farm at Langton Matravers and Dorchester Museum.

When July and First School Sports Day came, the weather was so hot that all the children were protected with sun tan lotion and encouraged to wear a shady hat.

When school broke up for the Summer holidays, the children were happy to present Mr Simon Bridges (Deputy Head) and Miss Elizabeth Vye with a coffee cafetière and salt & pepper mills on the occasion of their Wedding on 22 July. The Staff's gift was a Royal Doulton vegetable dish.

After the sunniest and driest Summer on record, school resumed with staff as follows: Mr A.N. Kellaway (Headmaster), Mr S. Bridges (Deputy Head: Science/Technology), Mr A. Cobb (Year 7 - I.T. AVA, French, Maths, Room G5), Mrs P. Searley (Year 6 - Health, Room F1), Mrs E. Bridges née Vye (Year 5 - Humanities Assessment, Room F5), Mrs C. Whish (Year 4 - English, Library, Room F2), Miss G. Tubbs (Year 3, Room F3), Miss T. Ligema (Year 2 - Dance, Room G4), Mrs A. Barton (Year 1 - Art/Display, Room G2), Mrs C. Oliver (Year R - English, R.E., Room G3), Mrs S. Davey (Nursery, Room G1), Miss Y. Cavell (NNEB), Mrs L. Carter (Secretary), Mrs C. Boulton (Assistant Secretary), Mrs M. Longden, Mrs L. Lowe SEN, Mrs J. Wilson SEN (Ancilliary Welfare Assistants), Mr R. Palmer (Caretaker), Mrs G. Hayes, Mrs F. Whitehead, Mrs S. Vine, Mrs P. Install (Lunch–time supervisory assistants).

Temporary Governing Bodies were set up for both the new Tatnam Farm Middle School (not necessarily the eventual name) and the replacement school at South Road (name still to be decided at the time of writing). When fully established, the Governors will be responsible for appointing the Heads and teaching staff of both schools (as well as Oakdale School which is also involved in the transfer to Tatnam Farm).

Towards the end of 1995 discussions took place between Poole Headteachers' Group and Poole Borough Council as the latter will resume responsibility for education (and other county services) in April 1997. The establishment of the unitary authority so close to the proposed date of South Road's move to Tatnam Farm seemed to suggest that the new Borough Council (which will resume the historic title of Borough and County of the Town of Poole') will have the almost immediate task of taking responsibility for refurbishing the existing South Road building ready for its proposed use as a First school.

Time for South Road School, a well respected and much loved institution, was fast running out as the year 1995 came to an end.

We can only hope that whatever takes its place will not lose touch with the fine traditions which went before and that some of the magic of South Road is carried over to the Tatnam Farm School, whatever it may be called, in 1997.

Poole Secondary School

Surname: Christopher Christian Names: Mabel Sex: Female No. 21

Name of Father or Guardian: James F. Christopher Postal Address: Post Office, Lytchett Minster, Poole

1. Date of Birth.			8. Place of Residence.	9. Occupation of Father.	10. Place or places of previous education during the two years preceding
Day 27	Month 3	Year 91	County Borough or County Dorsetshire and		Hamworthy Council School
2. Date of Admission.			(a) Borough or	Sub. Postmaster	
Day 14	Month 10	Year 04	(b) Urban District or		
3. Date of Leaving.			(c) Rural Parish Lytchett Minster		
Day 31	Month 7	Year 09	11. Particulars of any exemption from Tuition fees.	12. Particulars of any Public Examinations passed or Certificates obtained while in the School, with dates.	13. Date of Recognition as Bursar or P.T. in the School.

	(a) Total exemption.	(b) Partial exemption.		
4. Position on Admission. 1st Year Form	Granted from (Date).	Granted from (Date). May 1905	Inorg Chem. St 1. Cl 2. 1906 Prelim. Cat. 1909.	Bursar.
5. Position on Leaving. Senr P.T.	Granted by (Body awarding).	Granted by (Body awarding). Dorset County Council		Pupil-Teacher. Aug 1 1907
6. Boarder or Day-Scholar. Day	Tenable for	Annual Amount £1-11-6 Tenable for 2 years & 1 term		

7. Terms kept.		
Autumn	Spring	Summer
1904	1905	1905
1905	1906	1906
1906	1907	1907
1907	1908	1908
1908	1909	1909

14. Scholarships or Exhibitions for further education.	15. Place of further education.	16. Occupation taken up after leaving.	17. Remarks.
		Assistant mistress	

Staff: Poole Grammar School 1907. Standing Rev'd H. S. Maguire, Mr. J.F.L. Bohs, Mr. Green, Mr. Thomas, Mr. Evans. Seated: Miss M. K. Oliver, Miss E.M. Leir, Mr. Mockridge (Head), Miss Ramsbotton, Miss Glassey.

Poole Grammar School

As the twentieth century dawned, attention turned to the way every child, rich or poor, could develop fully - in other words secondary education. Whereas elementary schools, whether voluntary or provided, had relied on pupil-teachers, these were now encouraged to go to training college after a secondary education. Poole was lucky that Dorset County Council soon shirked its new responsibility for secondary education under the 1902 Education Act and delegated it to the Borough. A Secondary School was firmly on its Education Committee's agenda. At the same time a rival endeavour was being mounted in Parkstone, based on the Colet Institute and backed by church resources, which led to some friction.

Dorset County Council, encouraged by grants from Government windfall liquor duties, had established a technical school and pupil-teacher centre in the Library in Mount Street, now the top end of Lagland Street, given to the Borough by teetotaller John J. Norton. As **Poole Technical and Commercial School** it commenced in 1902. On 19th September 1904, under Poole Borough Council, it opened as **Poole Secondary School** with Mr G. Boyer BA as Headmaster. It offered an education of a practical nature to boys and girls of 12 years of age and over. A wide range of subjects was listed, including shorthand, elocution and for girls only, gymnastics. It was housed at the top of the Free Library and in an adjoining house. From the windows high up in Mount Street a pleasant pastime for the girls was to watch the weddings taking place across the High Street at the Wesleyan (now called the Methodist) Church.

One of the first entrants was Grace Dorothy Hixson who entered as a P-T (Pupil-Teacher) from Swanage Council School on 4 years' engagement. Before she left in 1909 she had attained the position of Senior P.T. having passed her Preliminary Certificate with distinction in English and the Oxford Senior Locals. Another early entrant, George Butson from Wimborne Minster National School, went on to become an Assistant Master at Wimborne Minster Grammar School before becoming a detective in the Metropolitan Police Force.

The Mount Street school, catering for 30 pupils, was a temporary measure. It was overcrowded and had no playground or corporate life. Its uniform included a straw hat and the school colours were light blue and dark blue.

The Council was delighted when Lord Wimborne offered a free gift of

2 acres of land at Seldown for a new Secondary School but wrangles followed as Mr Brennand, a member of the Education Committee and founder of the rival Colet Institute at Ashley Cross in 1905 *(see later)*, attempted to torpedo the plans as an extravagance. All he achieved was that the cost of the new Poole Secondary School (£5,000 for building and £1,231.5s.0d. for furnishing) had to be met from rates rather than by loan, the hard working founders, Alderman Charles Carter, Chairman of the Education Committee, and Mr Boyer, Headmaster, resigned and the atmosphere was of animosity rather than pride. Resentment at the increase in rates to pay for it - a penny rate for higher education then raising £800 – and parsimony was to continue in the town for some years, compounded by the Campbell-Bannerman Government laying down in 1907 that all Local Education Authorities were to reserve at least 25% of their places at secondary schools for 'scholarship children' from elementary schools.

In January 1908 the Poole Secondary School building at Kingland Road, Seldown was completed and first occupied under a new Headmaster, Mr A.J. Mockridge MA. It had been designed to accommodate 200 pupils. The uniform included a gold and green cap.

When the Great War broke out in 1914 almost all the male staff enlisted. Mr Mockridge lost a son in battle and his name was listed with others remembered with pride on the War Memorial which graced the entrance (and has since been re-located to St James Churchyard at Poole). Each Armistice Day became doubly poignant as the Head read out all the names during the service of Thanksgiving. The pupils' war effort included collecting acorns for the production of nitro glycerine at Holton Heath. Plans to extend the school buildings were, of necessity, put on hold. But numbers of pupils increased rapidly, many travelling from outside the Town by train, and the curriculum widened.

It is recorded that in 1917, the Head Girl obtained a distinction in Greek in the Oxford Local. Just after World War I ended, fee-paying parents had to find £12 a year to send their children to Poole Secondary, even though it was in the shadow of the Gas Works. As one wag wrote, *"Up to yon massive gassy plant/Our border doth abide/And we must thank our sainted aunt/It doesn't come inside"*.

The Hadow Report of 1927 envisaged that secondary modern' schools would be established, from which grammar schools would be distinguished. With the depression and a tight fiscal situation this reorganisation was to take Poole more than ten years to achieve.

In 1927 the children welcomed their new Grammar School Status and a casket representing the old Secondary School was carried in procession to the playing fields at the rear of the school where a 'burial ceremony' was enacted, involving a youthful Herbert C.R. Ballam (later to become Mayor and a Freeman of the Borough) as the 'Very Irrelevant Bishop of Seldown'.

Mr Mockridge continued as Head until 1927 when Mr A.W.M. Greenfield took over. This gentleman, in addition to his academic

1925 – Mr. Mockridge (Head) seated centre with Mr. Thomas (Deputy Head) (R) and Miss Bartle (L). Together with School Prefects. Note junior pupils getting into the picture – background (R).

qualifications had been decorated with the Legion d'Honneur and the Belgian Croix de Guerre. He continued as Headmaster until 1950.

Despite the fact that at this time there were neither files nor telephones at school, in 1928 the first School Magazine was produced. It contained no illustrations but was the forerunner of what was to become an important feature of the School Year encompassing every aspect of School Life from the House Performances, Sports achievements, social clubs and contributions from present and past pupils. It was during this period too that an expanded vision of Sixth Forms manifested, resulting in many boys being well prepared for University life.

1925 – 1st XI Hockey Team.

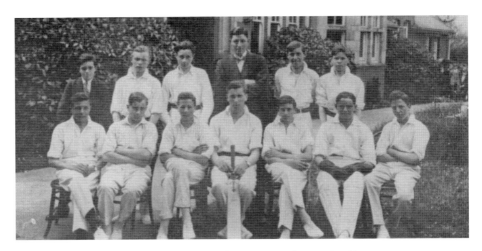

1925 – 1st XI Cricket Team, with Mr. Gould.

The School continued happily as a co-educational establishment with the addition of a quadrangle in 1931 and the central clock tower the following year until the end of 1937 when past disputes were resolved and Parkstone Grammar School *(see later)* at Ashley Cross took all female students and Poole became a boys' only school, taking over Seldown House as an extension.

Not everyone agreed with this re-arrangement but the Second World War started in September 1939 causing further disruption. Not least was the necessity to share premises with the King Edward VI School from Southampton which meant staggered morning/afternoon occupation as well as Saturday School Days. Brick built Air Raid Shelters were eventually erected round the Quad area but as a temporary measure trenches were dug for that purpose at the side of the tennis courts. Despite everything the academic achievements remained high.

The 1944 Education Act made all secondary education in state maintained schools free. Mr F.H. Stevens became Head on 11 September 1950 around the time when the old School Certificate was being replaced by a simpler General Certificate of Education (GCE) The final transition took place the following year.

The Debating Society of the school in November of 1950 had as their subject the motion *"That the Law should be amended, with simple precautions, to make it possible to end by painless means the life of a person suffering from an incurable disease"* – an issue still unsolved and still being debated. That it was noted then as a lively and 'amusing' debate is puzzling but anyway the motion was defeated by 39 to 28 votes.

The great event of 1951 was the Festival of Britain celebrated on the South Bank of the Thames. 400 boys visited in July 1951 and were impressed by the Skylon and The Dome of Discovery.

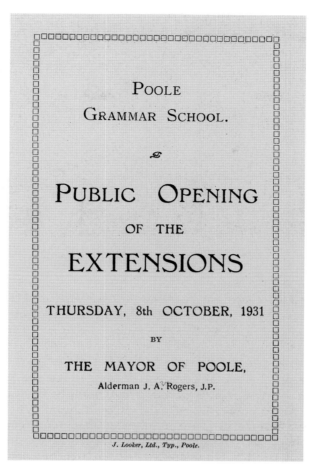

POOLE
GRAMMAR SCHOOL.

PUBLIC OPENING

OF THE

EXTENSIONS

THURSDAY, 8th OCTOBER, 1931

BY

THE MAYOR OF POOLE,

Alderman J. A. Rogers, J.P.

J. Looker, Ltd., Typ., Poole.

During the building of these extensions, the 'Annexe' (actually an ex-Army corrugated iron shed erected in 1919 and divided into four classrooms – J, M, N, V,) was removed piece by piece during school lessons. The quadrangle, Art Room and extra classrooms were also added at that time.

The Annual Circus held on the adjacent Ladies' Walking Field was especially inviting this year with elephants, midgets, lions and cowboys and the added attraction of a single Llama.

The opening of the school tuck shop was welcomed by the boys but was classed as a *"celebration of sorts"* by some who described it as a slightly shabby shed. Another innovation at that time was the formation of a Poole Old Grammarians' Association.

Due to lack of space at School, Speech Days had to be held in the Regent Cinema in High Street which was opposite the turning into Seldown Road in those days. The School Amateur Dramatic Society used Parkstone Girls' Great Hall for most productions. In November 1953 *'The Pirates of Penzance'*

Top: 1939 – The 'Quad' before the war.

1940 – The 'Quad' with air raid shelters. Note the High Street Regent Cinema and the Seldown Round houses (L) background.

was performed to a packed audience there. The Producer was Edna Tice and the musical director Mr Tristram. The School magazine reported that member of staff Mr Gill gave a polished performance as Major General Stanley and pupil Anthony Kellaway (later to become Head of South Road School) played *"a handsome and tender lover, Frederic."* Due praise was given to all the beautiful young girls of cast and chorus. Whoever would have mistaken them for pupils of Poole Boys' Grammar School?

Preparing the rough land at the back of the school to provide a Field Athletics Area was helped along by boys who were sent there to work in lieu of detentions. The Official Opening was held on 9 June 1954.

It was Mr N.J. Cleave who had taken over as Headmaster in 1954 , the year of the School's 50th Anniversary, who was due to oversee the move from Seldown to a brand new complex on Gravel Hill. Owing to his indisposition the running of the school during a great deal of the transition period was taken over by Mr Whitelock, the Senior School Chemistry Master. The work of building the new School was entrusted to Poole Borough Council's Works Department and cost £327,000. The Seldown site was to be taken over by Seldown School (see later).

The official opening ceremony of the newly built grammar school buildings was performed by HRH Princess Margaret on 11 October 1966. For the first time in 30 years Speech Day on 15 March 1967 could be held on the school premises in the new school hall.

With a brand new school surrounded by playing fields, tennis courts, and ample car parking, much effort was now put into introducing educational measures long dreamed of. Up-to-date methods of teaching languages, mathematics and science were able to be practiced. And the school soon established its own radio transmitting station.

The Parents' and Staff Association as well as the Old Grammarians' Association flourished and by the time Mr John Cleave retired in 1972 after eighteen years as Headmaster the range of extra-curricular activities was vast. In addition to the Rugby, Football, Cricket and Tennis Teams, there were Athletics, swimming, squash, volleyball, basketball, computer, stamp, dancing, chess, table tennis and cross country clubs all thriving at Poole Grammar. Also there were Societies for Chemistry, World Wildlife, Sixth Form Stock Exchange, Railway, Photographic, Natural History, Music, Model-making, Film, Electronics, Astronomy, Debating and Archaeology. For a time there was a Craft Gild so named (and spelt) from an organisation of the 12th and 13th century which encouraged craftwork.

Mr Nigel J. Gilpin took over the Headship from Mr Cleave in 1972 until December 1988 when Mr J. Wheway, already Deputy Head since 1986 became Acting Head (apart from the two terms served by Mr Haydn J. Adams for Spring and Summer 1989) until July 1990.

During 1988 the new General Certificate of Secondary Education Exam (GCSE) was introduced to replace the GCE General Certificate of Education O' and A' levels and the CSE (Certificate of Secondary Education) exams.

1953 – All-boy cast of 'Pirates of Penzance' on stage.

Around the same time the National Curriculum was being introduced. All schools were obliged to apply National Tests to scholars at ages seven, eleven, fourteen and sixteen, the four Key Stages, to assess attainment levels. Parents could exercise their right to send children to schools of their choice and schools were allowed to opt out of local authority control.

One of the highlights of 1989 was the performance of Poole Grammar School Stompers at the *'Last Night of The School Proms'* in the Albert Hall. They had been the toast of the promenaders then, and at a Gala Charity Concert at the Wessex Hall at Poole Arts Centre in June of 1990, they again rendered such numbers as *'Bad'* and *'Confusion'*. The programme was indeed varied and Liszt's *'Transcendental Study No. 4 in D Minor'* was performed by Raymond Clarke, now a successful professional concert pianist, who as a pupil 15 years previously had shown great promise. The concert, attended by the Mayor and Sheriff raised in excess of £2,000 for the Motor Neurone Disease Association.

In July of 1990 Mr Alex Clarke became Head.

The School had 700 pupils, all there by parental choice. The 6th Form was thriving and the School Grant Maintained, in charge of its own budget, no longer paid by the Dorset County Council but in effect employees of the School Governors.

The Old Boys' Association took over full financing of the school magazine, *'The Dolphin'*, published since 1928, and this thanks mainly to the efforts of Mr N.G. Latcham, Biology Master and head of the Upper Main School. He was a previous pupil and is proud of the fact that he helped in the building and plumbing of the new school during his student holidays from University.

And again in 1993 (as they had in 1953) the Dramatic Society chose to perform *'Pirates of Penzance'*. This time though the girls taking part were

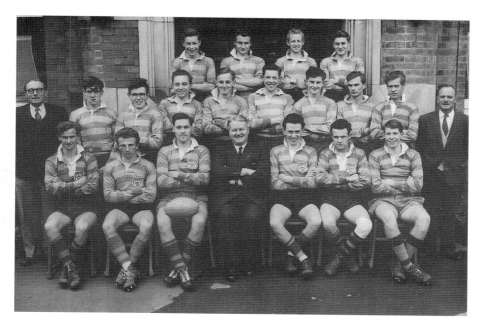

Top: 1959/60 – Rubgy Team with Mr. Cleave (Head) seated centre. Mr. Hopewell (L),
Mr. Waters (R).

1959/60 – Football Team with Mr. Cleave (Head) seated centre and
Mr. Hall (Physics Master) (R).

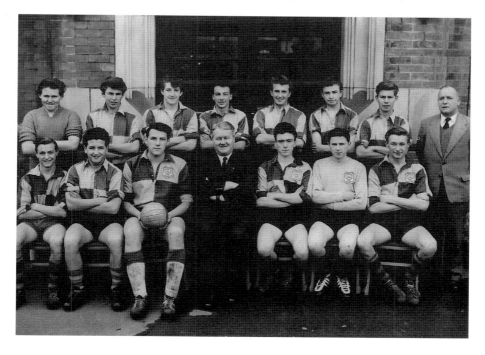

females from the Parkstone Grammar School and not prettily disguised Poole Boys. A sign of the times though was the comment that they were hardly recognisable out of their 'Doc Marten' heavy shoes!

Out of school activities continued apace and foreign trips came thick and fast during 1994. In February a ski trip to Austria. Easter saw the Italian Grand Tour (including the Leaning Tower of Pisa). In June a French exchange took place and work experience was gained both at home and in France. There were various activities weeks in this country and a Geography Field Trip by some 6th formers to the Brecon Beacons.

In July of 1995 the school hit the TV news by being taken over for a day as a Police Station. Junior boys enacted situations that arise daily in the pursuit of law and order.

And so the broad range of mental and physical experiences continues, aimed at bringing out the best in all boys attending Poole Grammar School.

FINIS OPUS CORONAT

1988 – St. James Church, Poole. Mr. J. Wheway, President, laying the wreath at the Rededication Service following the re-siting of the War Memorial.

168

Henry Harbin School

H enry Harbin School was built in 1938 on a large site behind Poole Fire Station and the Stadium, formerly 'Whittle's Field'. Its playing fields were bordered at one end by the Tatnam Road houses and by the railway line and Sterte Road houses along the side.

At one time there was a suggestion the new school be named the Wimborne Road Senior but thanks largely to the intervention of Alderman Herbert Carter it became the Henry Harbin School bearing the name of a benefactor (a free Burgess of Poole in 1701) who, on his death two years later, bequeathed a grand sum (£200) as an educational endowment, used latterly to provide School Prizes, under the name Harbin Trust.

Henry Harbin Senior School was opened officially on Wednesday May 3rd 1939 by The Right Honourable, the Earl of Shaftesbury, KP, GCVO, CBE, Lord Lieutenant of the Counties of Dorset and Poole, in the presence of the Mayor of Poole, Councillor Joe Bright.

The school accommodated children from the age of 11. Mr H.P. Smith from South Road became Head of the Boys' Department and the girls had Miss G.M. Harding from St James' as Headmistress.

In addition to sixteen classrooms this new school sported large assembly halls, laboratories, Arts and Crafts rooms and specially equipped workrooms for Wood and Metal work instruction. The girls were well served with Domestic Science and Housecraft rooms. In addition, an extensive library, founded in part from the Harbin Trust. Nowadays the main aim of the Trust is the provision of library books.

Very *avant-garde* at the time was the ciné projector and classroom amplifiers. The resultant reception of wireless broadcasts and gramophone reproductions direct to the classrooms enhanced music and literature lessons.

Unfortunately, before the school had settled in properly World War II broke out on 3rd September 1939, exactly 4 months after the opening.

Immediately the children filled sandbags at the near-by Fire Station to help protect the school from the blast from bombs which were expected any time. In the event this didn't happen until the following year.

Air Raid Shelters were built along the front of the school. In deference to the necessity to save paper, the new school magazine had to be abandoned after one issue and a News Bulletin was issued periodically in its place. Waste paper and metal collections were arranged at once for the War Effort and two

A brand new Henry Harbin School ready of occupation, 1938 The main entrance.

large bins were set up near the entrance gate plainly marked 'Bones Collection'.

All these things were sold and raised 55 guineas for the Mayor of Poole's Spitfire Fund.

Later, the School Sports Fund benefited from some of the proceeds. In 1940 there was a problem in getting the new Playing Field grass cut by the Corporation workmen, so that when a local farmer offered to graze his sheep there, the idea was welcomed. It was reported at one time 200 sheep were munching away not only keeping the grass down but also fertilizing the soil. (News Bulletin, December 1940).

The four Houses Jolliffe, Haviland, Longspee and Thompson vied fiercely with each other on the sports field and found the evacuees from Stockwell Road vigorous opponents.

After the war H.P. Smith was succeeded by Mr E.H. Smith. In June 1948 the Girls' School was visited by the Rt. Hon. George Tomlinson MP, Minister of Education. He also visited other Schools in Dorset and the new County School Camp at Carey near Wareham which had been set up on Hardy's Egdon Heath and is still much used today.

In June of 1955 the girls' school staged a Home Craft Exhibition. Classrooms were set out and furnished in the up-to-the-minute fashion. Handwork and embroidery of a very high standard was displayed in what at the time of writing is the library. Dolls were dressed and clothes made by the girls were modelled by them at a Fashion Parade. It was, in a way, a 'grand

1946 – Sports Day. A group of budding sportsmen posing on the playing field site at the rear of the school.

Henry Harbin Girls' School Play, 'The Merchant of Venice' 1947/48. Cast: Sybil Shapiro, Margaret Phillips, Anne Lewis, Rosemary Brown, Sheila Loader, Sylvia Smith, Sylvia Jones.

finale' to Miss Harding's 32 years of Headship in Poole, (16 years at St. James' before her 16 years at Henry Harbin). On her retirement in September 1955 good wishes and tributes flooded in from all quarters. Miss Garrard then became Headmistress of the Girls' school and R.A. Pearce M.A., B.Sc. took

June 1948 – Henry Harbin Girls' School Exhibition of Home Crafts. Display of post-war lounge furniture together with girls embroidered chair-backs, tablecloths etc. Note the quadrangle through the classroom windows and the lovely Poole Pottery flower vases on the tables inside.

over the Headship of the Boys in 1960.

A pupil of the Boys' school won the Poole Schools Competition, 'Road Safety Week at Schools, 1962' with an essay warning of the danger of the increasing number of cars coming on the roads. What vision that pupil had!

In 1963 President John Kennedy of the United States of America was assassinated and the school was as stunned and saddened as were all young people of the Western World to whom he symbolised the path of conciliation with Russia, and a hope to the end of the Cold War.'

Mr Pearce was keen that his boys strove hard to gain academic achievement. They worked to obtain GCE and CSE certficates and many having attained suitable grades were able to continue their studies in the Grammar School's 6th Form. Others attended Poole College to gain necessary qualifications to pursue worthwhile careers. Pastimes were not neglected for the school ran an orchestra (augmented at times by the girls) and choir. They produced Gilbert & Sullivan evenings, visited the Bournemouth Symphony Orchestra regularly as members of the Wessex Musical Society and were encouraged to participate on stage at the Annual Speech Days held at the

Henry Harbin Girls' School – June 1948. A classroom display of reproduction Jacobean dining furniture, courtesy of Bealesons Store which was then situated in Commercial Road, Bournemouth just above Marks and Spencer.

Regent Cinema in Poole High Street and in the School Hall.

A grant from the Ministry of Works was forthcoming in 1963 to assist in the Archaeological work to unearth Roman Relics.

And sport was certainly on the agenda too, with hockey, boxing and judo. The junior cross-country running team won the local event in 1963 and the third-year soccer team won the League Cup. That same year, the captain of the County Junior Rugger XV was a Harbin boy.

By 1971 all children were obliged to remain at school until 16 years of age, and to accommodate the increase in numbers a new 5th year block was opened in front of the original school to accommodate them. It was in 1972 that Mr R.J. Mealings took over as Head of the **Combined** schools.

Over the years, the school expanded almost out of recognition with the addition of Art and Drama Studios, new staffrooms, Science laboratories and Home Economics and Technology Rooms. Overseas holidays became the norm and the school encouraged its pupils to participate in the Duke of Edinburgh's Award Scheme. Educational standards have kept abreast of changing government requirements over the years. In 1990 the National

Henry Harbin Girls' Secondary Modern School, June 1948.
The Rv. Hon. George Tomlinson M.P. Minster of Education viewing work
to be exhibited later that month at school.

Curriculum core subjects were Maths and Science since when other core subjects such as Modern Languages have been introduced into the timetable.

Under the headship of Mr Short who took over in September 1986, the school became Grant Maintained in April 1993. It is classified a bilateral/technical school and according to details released mid-1995 its Standard Number is 240 students. Intakes at 12+ is higher, approximately 275 students each year, and the Senior School (6th Form) exceeds 200.

Henry Harbin was re-named **Poole High School** (called affectionately by many as Poole Tech High) much to the dismay of many who regret the disappearance of the Harbin name, which was so significant during the early days of schooling and yet another link lost with the colourful history of a wonderful old town.

Parkstone Grammar School

Parkstone Girls' Grammar School now stands on a fine open site incorporating vast playing fields at Soper's Lane. It boasts its own swimming pool, fitness rooms, technology rooms, Language Centre, Drama Studio, a minibus, and is a far cry from its predecessor at Ashley Cross. There the Great Hall doubled as a gymnasium; classrooms were scattered along its side and up around twisted stairs all over the building. The carved oak double entrance doors were always a feature and are to be preserved for posterity. Their eventual fate is not known at the time of writing. They led into a hall to the left of which in the early days was one staff room, Secretary's office (Miss Hill) and the Domestic Science Room. On the other side was a Staff room, one of many stairways, the entrance to a cloakroom and, just before entering the great hall the original school kitchen.

The Prep' School for mixed juniors was accommodated in a converted pair of semi-detached houses situated in the Oaks' grounds at the back of the school.

To play tennis the girls were obliged to visit East Dorset Tennis Club in Salterns Road and the playing field on Constitution Hill Road was used for hockey.

The school at Ashley Cross was originally built by Mr William Ernest Brennand as Church House (later the front part of Ashley Cross School) which he loaned to St Peter's rent fee for five years. Mr Brennand then decided that Parkstone should have its own Secondary School for boys and girls and built the **Colet Institute** behind Church House. He offered it to the Education Committee for use as a Secondary School and when they declined it, he opposed the plan for a school at Seldown (*see Poole Grammar School*), opened his own school, naming it the **Parkstone School.** The prospectus was issued in November 1904 and the school opened on 24 January 1905 to accommodate 14 children aged 9 and above, both boys and girls. The Vicar of St Peter's, Revd Stanley Moss, was also Headmaster. It developed as a voluntary fee paying day and boarding school, but ran into financial trouble in 1913, when Mr Brennand died, leaving the school mortgaged.

Although heavily in debt and unable to offer free places except through private donations as Poole Education Committee would not support it, immediately after the First World War the school began to expand rapidly and in 1922 the space between the two original buildings was roofed over to

Parkstone School Main Entrance c1923
In 'Tudor Style', brick with sandstone detailing. Stone mullioned windows and prominently featured Terracotta chimney stacks (probably made by the local George Jennings Pottery). In 1952 the crumbling sandstone was removed and the entire frontage covered in brickwork. The porch was taken away and the windows replaced in the modern style. The double oak doors were preserved in 1995 when the building was demolished.

The Great Hall

become the Great Hall.

Under the headship of the Reverend E. Stanley Moss the school thrived academically, but financial problems were not resolved until Dorset County Council resolved Poole Council's intransigence by taking it over in 1935, with Mr Moss remaining as Headmaster.

The School ran as a mixed concern for a short time after Miss W.M. Allen became Headmistress in April 1937. At the end of that year, all male pupils and staff were transferred to Poole Grammar School, and Parkstone became a **Girls' Grammar School**. It was at that point that scholarship children from the elementary schools were allowed in on a non-paying basis.

Not everyone was pleased with the arrangements. Long it had been a local saying *'Poole for brains, Parkstone for manners'* and many wished it to stay that way.

However, Miss Allen, a wondrous Christian lady guided the transition smoothly and then had the added burden of World War II to contend with, the school becoming a reception area for evacuees. Her memories are of them all arriving complete with gas mask and a tin of bully beef plus a paper carrier containing all their possessions. The numbers which had already been rising rapidly topped 500 at this time. Summer holiday terms were introduced, for not many went off on holiday. They were in reality great fun, for the few lessons were enhanced by many activities not entered into during normal school terms. For example play acting, elocution and handcrafts such as the making of papier-mache puppets. Even Esperanto was introduced.

I remember an incident when my great pal Mary (Mamie) Taylor and I had managed to persuade others of our class to join us on a flat roof which was reached by climbing out of a stairway window which looked down directly on to the playground below. We got away with it for almost a week and then one day the duty Mistress, Miss Barnes spied us from below. Mamie and I realised the game was up and scrambled back inside and hid in a large games cupboard on the landing. We thought we were safe and had no idea where the others had scarpered when the door of the cupboard was thrown open and an extremely angry Miss Barnes shouted "Get Out and Report to Miss Allen.".

Lining up in the Entrance Hall ready to be summoned upstairs into the Headmistress's room were eight of us, one of whom was a girl called Joyce Foxall. Typically, (and she wouldn't deny it), she fell backwards whilst waiting and plonked her behind into one of the Fire Buckets which were always filled to capacity with water in case of incendiary bombs landing on the school. Mamie and I dashed into the Domestic Science Room for mopping up cloths and so were able to hide our intense mirth as we, on hands and knees made feeble attempts to dry the floor. By the time it was our turn to stand before Miss Allen I think any anger had been spent and she seemed to see the funny side too. However, we never ventured on to that roof again.

The Silver Jubilee year of the school was celebrated on 7th January 1955, and coincidentally the Jubilee sermon was preached by a Revd Moss (W.H.

Single desks, well spaced.

Osmond Moss). He began by recalling the St. Commemorative Day Service of the school which had been held in the same Church (St Peter's) on 27 January 1909 when the school was only 4 years old and had already grown from 14 to 150 pupils.

The 21st year of Miss Allen's Headship, 1958, coincided with the new school site being chosen at Fleetsbridge. She retired in December of 1959 and a new Headmistress, Miss M.L. McGuiness was appointed to take over the new Soper's Lane School in 1960.

It was Miss Allen however who had the honour of laying its foundation stone in April of that year. But it was not until over a year later that the school was really ready for occupation. In the interim period the old Ashley Cross building in addition to the Torvaine Building in St Peter's road had to be shared with the new secondary School.

Nearly a year after the official move to the new site, the Rt. Hon. Sir David Eccles KCVO, MP, Minister for Education, officially opened it on 9 July 1962.

Miss McGuiness was Headmistress during the period the Borough reorganised its schools into First, Middle and Secondary. She retired in 1976 (writing a history of the school in 1980) and was followed by Mrs C. Birchett. In 1979 Miss Allen died. All her schooldays were a testament to the forward she wrote in the school magazine in 1956:- *"The record of any school must in the end be built upon the lives, the personalities and the achievements of people. Whatever bricks and mortar, paper and ink, machines, apparatus, instruments and aids man may provide, it is in the end, the human thought, will and action that makes a school."*

1914 – Rev'd Stanley Moss Headmaster in his study.

1914 – Parkstone School Staff. Rev'd Stanley Moss seated cente.

When Mrs Birchett retired, Parkstone was still, despite many qualms to the contrary, a Grammar School and not a Comprehensive. Dr Paula Haes took up the reins in April 1987. She has brought enlightenment in a rapidly changing world. The school has become Grant Maintained and much new building has ensued. Aided by the girls themselves and Kriss Akabussi a new multi-gym was built. The technology department was updated and an International Language Centre added. A well equipped Drama Studio behind the main hall was opened in March 1995.

And of course, the girls too are updated. No longer the black pleated gymslips and velour hats in Winter, nor the yellow, red or green checked dressed with white collars and a panama in Summer.

The School celebrated its 90th Anniversary in 1995 and Dr Haes was justly proud of its continuing academic achievements. Plans for a purpose built Sixth Form Centre were already well under way with the prospect of additional seminar rooms as well.

The prospect is indeed bright for the superb Parkstone Girls' Grammar School which has its roots in the love and caring attitude of one Parkstone Gentleman.

Parkstone School 1914. Master taking mixed class for Chemistry. Note the gas light behind him and the 'Eton' collars worn by the boys.

1962 – The New Parkstone Grammar School, Poole.
Inset: 1995 – Present Head Dr. Paula Haes.

Domestic Science

1961 – The new Ashley Cross Secondary School notice is prominently displayed. Only the entrance doors remain of the original school frontage and these were preserved in 1995 when the building was demolished to make way for a housing development.
(Courtesy of Marion Watson).

Ashley Cross Girls' School

Because the move by Parkstone Grammar School to its new site at Soper's Lane was behind schedule the newly formed Secondary Modern Ashley Cross Girls' School was obliged to use the Torvaine building, a large house in grounds on the corner of North Road and St Peter's Road (at the time of writing the Eagle House Independent School) during the early part of 1961 as a temporary measure until it took over the main Ashley Cross building just before Christmas.

The rooms allocated as classrooms were small, and for the most part could accommodate up to 20 girls only. One of the larger rooms was used for morning assembly with desks and chairs having to be stacked out of the way before and replaced each time after it was used.

Because there was no dining room, the girls' desks had to double up' as dinner tables. Apparently this was the reason so many exercise books sported gravy stains. However, despite this, the food was pronounced first-class – possibly on account of the copious helpings of ice-cream which served as sweet most days.

Lessons quite frequently over-ran. There was no electric bell from an office and the teacher whose duty it happened to be to ring the hand-bell was often pre-occupied with her teaching.

However despite the restrictions of Torvaine it was with mixed feeling that the girls eventually filed down St Peter's Road to take up occupancy of the School buildings newly vacated by the Parkstone Grammar Girls.

Miss G.F. Ashurst ARCM was the first Headmistress, with a teaching staff of seven at the outset and 130 girls from the catchment areas of Canford Cliffs, Sandbanks, Lilliput, Branksome and Lower Parkstone.

The new school uniform was predominantly red. Cherry red berets, navy blue blazer with red piping, a navy skirt, white blouse and red jumper. Knee length cherry red socks completed the outfit. In addition to the usual academic subjects, Art, needlework and Domestic Science were given prominence. The need to accommodate these subjects satisfactorily resulted in additional classrooms being built in the back Oaks area and by October 1965 these were ready for occupation.

Two double classrooms were converted for Home Economics (Housecraft) use and two temporary classrooms erected on the front lawn. The attic rooms became out-of-bounds after a Fire Inspection which resulted in the Library, which had been housed on the top floor, being brought downstairs into the old Housecraft Room. And then to accommodate the extra children compelled from 1971 to continue their education until 16 years of age, a 5th year ROSLA block was erected on the remains of the Oaks orchard.

Miss Mulrain took over as Headmistress in 1974 (Audrey Quick being her deputy), and with numbers still increasing classrooms at the rear of the old St Peter's School were taken over for a time.

By 1977 the fifth year had grown from 90 girls to 140. The old School building was by then surrounded by a hotch-potch of extensions and additions which covered the side lawn and most of the old Oaks at the back. It had become fragmented and difficult to administer.

The School had served the local community well over the years, but the time had come to move on and in 1988 that's just what Ashley Cross did, with Mrs M. Snell as Head.

Joined by boys from Seldown School they reverted to a mixed Secondary establishment at the new **Ashdown School** on Canford Heath.

Alas, true to what seemed to have become the norm during transition, work was behind schedule and although Ashdown functioned as a combined site for the year of 1987 it was in fact being run from the two separate schools. It is surprising, that, given the circumstances, more disruption to classwork was not experienced, for the teaching staff had to travel back and forth between Seldown and Ashley Cross for some lessons.

But eventually both schools moved into Ashdown and Ashley Cross reverted to being part of a mixed-sex educational establishment as it had been at its inception in 1905.

By 1995 the old school buildings and all the extensions had been demolished and a new housing development and Probation Office began to cover the site. The original Parkstone School front doors, alone, had been boarded up on site ready to be preserved as a reminder of the past entrance to learning and achievement.

Seldown School

Seldown Secondary Modern School was so named because it took over the site of Poole Grammar School incorporating Seldown House at the far end of the then Ladies' Walking Field. Seldown Bridge and Dolphin Pool are situated in the same area at the time of writing.

The school opened in September 1966 with Mr Peter F. Speed as Headmaster. He had moved into the area from Leicestershire where he had held the appointment of Deputy Head. Mr Speed was to serve Seldown with care and competence for seventeen years. He retired in December 1983 and from 1984 the Deputy Head, Mr Clive Cole became Acting Head until the merger with Ashley Cross as Ashdown (see later). He then reverted to Deputy Head, in conjunction with Mrs Sleat from Ashley Cross under the Headteacher Mrs M. Snell.

The school took pupils from the surrounding Junior Schools at Longfleet, St Peter's, Baden Powell, St Aldhelm's, Courthill and a few from South Road. The catchment areas actually covered Lilliput, Lower Parkstone and Upper Parkstone to the Ashley Road.

The traditional curriculum served the 500 plus pupils to O' Level standards in the GCE and CSE exams. The lower school classes were not streamed and contained pupils of mixed abilities which seemed to work well and children on leaving Seldown were well guided to pursue the occupations deemed most suitable.

Most pupils and staff considered the regime strict but fair and Seldown was in the vanguard of new innovations such as Year Heads whereby the entire year of classes, certainly up to the fifth, had its own separate head of year with Mr Speed in charge overall.

Presumably because the Headmaster's study was directly off the multi-purpose assembly hall and gymnasium and was therefore in line for a deal of noise and distraction, it had at some time been equipped with a rather unique double door. The outside of the first door had been covered in a green felt material (the green of Poole Grammar School boys) and seems to be a lasting memory of many pupils.

The uniform was black or dark grey trousers, black jacket with white or school grey shirt and a horizontally striped tie in blue and silver grey.

During 1987 whilst Ashdown was functioning as one school but still occupying the Ashley Cross and Seldown buildings, teaching staff often had to travel between the two buildings during the course of the day. It was

View of Seldown School taken from the roof of the Poole Arts Centre. Note the new housing development at Baiter (right – distant) and the swimming pool building behind.

sometimes necessary to use taxis to minimise the time lapses between classes.

Just in time, the hurricanes of October 1987 brought down trees in the School grounds next to the playing fields, unearthing a veritable treasure trove of turn-of-the-century artefacts such as bottles, pottery (including part of a dolls' tea set), rings and pieces of old railway track.

Because the school was due for demolition the boys were given permission to dig as much as they liked in order to find as much as possible. A special Archaeology Club was set up to help them identify their finds and much research went on at the local library.

It was therefore with mixed feelings, Seldown learned that Ashdown was ready for occupation in 1988. The excitement at moving out to a brand new purpose-built modern school was tinged for most with sadness too, at leaving a much loved Seldown. The premises had served Poole well over the years and would shortly be demolished to form part of the site of a new flyover.

Ashdown School

Ashdown School, situated within the fast-growing Canford Heath area was ready for occupation by the girls from Ashley Cross School and boys from Seldown School in September 1988, having been run as an entity from the two separate sites for the previous year.

The Headteacher was Mrs M. Snell from Ashley Cross and her deputies were Mr Clive Cole from Seldown and Mrs Pamela Sleat from Ashley Cross.

During the construction of the new building a Time Capsule was placed in a wall cavity within the 3-brick white band running round the red brick school walls. It contained items pertinent to 1988 chosen by 14 year old Alison Thomas and was not to be opened until the year 2088. These included a copy of the new National Curriculum, sets of coins and stamps, a school tie and strands of wool in the official school colours of black (skirts or trousers), white (tops) and red (jumpers). Copies of *The Times* and the *Sun* newspapers were also enclosed, together with computerised labelling and check-out receipts.

The School was opened officially on Friday 7 July 1989 by HRH The Princess Margaret, Countess of Snowdon.

The single storey school is well equipped with specialist rooms for Art & Design, Technology, Creative Textiles, Craft Design, Home Economics & Music. There are Drama and Dance Studios and fine Science laboratories in addition to 16 main base classrooms and a well equipped and much used library.

Great sadness was experienced when Mr Cole became terminally ill and after his death a memorial plaque was erected at school in his memory.

Mr T. Gillingham who was Head of Year of new intake in 1988 on Ashdown's opening and Mr K. Corio (Senior Teacher), both of whom had served Seldown School for its entire life, are still involved with Ashdown school at the time of writing, Mr Gillingham as a regular supply teacher and Mr Corio teaching music throughout the school..

Early on the school was included in the Educational Technology Award Scheme and outings to both Parliament and the House of Lords provided some of the pupils opportunity to observe the workings of the British System at first hand.

A new Headmaster, Mr Ashley Pellegrini, was appointed in the Summer of 1990 and has charge of a fast growing and energetic establishment. His

The Head, Mrs Mollie Snell, being presented to HRH The Princess Margaret
at the opening on July 7th.
Reproduced courtesy of the Bournemouth Evening Echo

deputy heads are Mrs P. Sleat and Dr K. Bawn.

The children have been encouraged to work for charity and a 'Day of Denim', when they were allowed for a 50p fee to wear other than school uniform, raised £225 for the British Diabetic Association in June 1995. Also, a former student, Steve Davies, severely injured in a motorcycle accident received a £700 gift towards a light-weight wheelchair.

The Canford Heath Beat Officer PC Mike Humphrey helped set up a Youth Action Group at school and the Dorset Police Video Unit filmed some of the pupils enacting aspects of Bullying and this was shown at a Youth Action Conference in Bristol.

At the time of writing, pupils of Year 10 and 11 are working on a theme Water & Movement' in advance of an exhibition to be staged at Poole Arts

The 'Time Capsule' being placed in the wall wall of the school during its construction.

Centre in 1996, sponsored by Wessex Water.

Signs of the times are highlighted in some of the rules included in the excellent School Handbook. For example it is laid down that hair should be a natural colour and not worn in an extravagant style. Nose-studs not allowed. Chewing gum, smoking, skateboards, aerosol cans and solvent-based substances strictly forbidden. Litter, both in school and out in the grounds not tolerated.

In 1995, Ashdown was proud to be one of only 223 schools awarded the Government's Charter Mark for excellence. Efforts on the part of staff and the 650 pupils succeeded in achieving a four hundred per cent improvement in its GCSE pass rates to raise it from its position in 1992 when it was near bottom of the school league table. A fine achievement.

BIBLIOGRAPHY

School Log Books & Magazines, Education Committee Minutes and local directories.

CONVERSION TABLE

12d = 1 shilling (1/-) = 5p

12 inches (″) = 1 foot (′) = 30.4 cms

20s = £1

10 sq ft = 0.929 sq metres

$1/3$ pint = 190 ml

1 acre = 0.4 hectares

INDEX of principal subjects and references